Your Guide to Successful Home Bible Studies

Your Guide to Successful Home Bible Studies

by
Norma Spande

Thomas Nelson Publishers
Nashville • New York

 Published in Nashville, Tennessee, by Thomas Nelson Inc., Publishers and simultaneously in Don Mills, Ontario, by Thomas Nelson & Sons (Canada) Limited. Manufactured in the United States of America.

Library of Congress Cataloging in Publication Data

Spande, Norma.
Your guide to successful home Bible studies.

1. Bible—Study. I. Title.
BS600.2.S67 220′.07 78-21036
ISBN 0-8407-5683-6

To the women in the first Bible study I attended
who, by their example of Christian love,
drew me to Him.

Eileen, Peggy, Marilyn, Helen, Joyce
Irma, Betty . . . and Kathy

Contents

Introduction

Have you heard? Are you aware of the epidemic sweeping across our nation? Twenty-five years ago it was rare, fifteen years ago unusual. But in the last five years it has grown to gigantic proportions.

Men, women, boys, and girls, all ages and nationalities, are gathering together in all manner of places to study and discuss—of all things—the Bible! They sit for hours, heads bent, eyes intent, on what? The Bible. They're all infected and are carriers of "Bible study itch."

Most of the time this itch can be scratched satisfactorily in a person's own home. But sometimes there may be complications requiring the tender care and counseling of others. When this happens people will drive or walk great distances in unusual weather conditions to meet with others and have the itch scratched by studying the Word. Criticism by friends and neighbors does little or nothing to halt the enthusiastic pursuit of this treatment.

There is no season for this prickly malady that spreads like "wildfire" year round. It can strike anyone, anytime; however, it is less common among those under age seven or over age ninety-nine.

A cure for Bible study "itchus" has never been found, and those who "suffer" with it are exceedingly grateful. Isolation is never recommended. For you see, the itch is really more similar to an appetite than a disease—an appetite that it feels so good to satisfy. The "afflicted" enjoy it and have no desire to be cured.

I suggest that you spend many hours in close contact with those who have it—if you're blessed, you may catch it too!

N.S.

Savage, Minnesota
Fall, 1978

CHAPTER 1

Getting in on the Explosion

I just came from a "new believers' " Bible study, and I'm so excited I can't settle down!

Just a few weeks ago the seven women involved were unbelieving, nervous, and skeptical. Today, each told how God is working in her life, how real He has become.

Three of these women are mothers who have led their children to the Lord. One mother, who has a problem child, shared her faith with her boy and he eagerly accepted Christ. Now he daily pours over his new Bible and shows an avid interest in spiritual matters.

Another woman's husband is now lovingly appreciative of her. They've been married eighteen years, and he has seldom shown any affection to her. But since she met the Lord he knows something is different; he doesn't understand it, but it's reaching him.

Acting on her Bible study assignment to do an act of kindness, another participant—Sharon—called her stepmother long distance. She found out the lady was scheduled for surgery the following day. Sharon made it clear that she loved and appreciated her. The next day the stepmother died in surgery. Later Sharon learned she was the only person in the study who had mistakenly done that lesson a week early.

A Leader! Who, Me?

You may be thinking of starting or leading a Bible study in your neighborhood, but you doubt that you're capable. There are many questions floating in your mind. As soon as one is answered, another bubbles up to keep you apprehensive. Do these sound familiar?

How can I lead when I've had no training?

Can I volunteer to lead without people thinking I'm setting myself up as an authority?

What will I do if someone asks a question I can't answer?

How do I choose a study?

How many people do I need to start, and where will I find them?

Where can I hold the study?

How do I begin?

What can I do if I want to be in a study, but I don't want to lead?

Does God ever ask us to do things we consider impossible? You bet He does. And as we respond to Him our faith grows. Scripture tells us that He's the enabler:

Now to him who by the power at work within us is able to do far more abundantly than all that we ask or think (Eph. 3:20)

Perhaps God is giving you a desire to serve Him in a home Bible study, but you're arguing with Him saying, "Who, me?"

Put aside your mental picture of yourself as "leader" and try to think of yourself as a tool that can be used in a variety of ways to reach others for Christ: hostess, leader, team-teacher, or babysitter. Be open to see the different ways you can be used. Choose one and step out in faith. Begin.

As a counselor I talk to many discouraged people who tell me they've had an urge to have a home Bible study but haven't because they don't measure up to their idea of what a leader should be. They feel disobedient to God because they haven't gone ahead with a study. When I ask them what they consider a good leader to be, they tell me, "Someone who has been a Christian for many years, a person trained in Bible school, and someone who has all the answers." At that I smile, because I know many leaders who don't fit that description at all.

God Uses the Humble

The leaders I know are average people, most of them fairly new Christians who have a living and growing relationship with Jesus Christ. They've found answers and direction from the Bible for their lives, and they want to help others find the same help. It's an astounding truth that God gives the average individual godly wisdom when that individual needs it and asks for it. The Bible has the answers to all our problems, but it's up to us to find and apply them.

One leader I know is, by the world's standards, uneducated. Her vocabulary is limited and she is a very "ordinary" person. Yet in her Bible study group she exceeds the others in her wisdom concerning God's ways and workings. She studies the Bible diligently and has learned to trust God. She has a peace in her life that others envy. She is used often to encourage and strengthen the faith of those whose education and personal status surpass hers. Her quiet, gentle, humble way is Christ-like. She is not a "leader type"; yet, because she is willing, God uses her to draw others to Himself.

Can You Sell Something You're Not Sold On?

A few years ago a salesman talked me into letting him demonstrate his aluminum cookware in our home by preparing and serving a meal for our family and a few friends.

He spent several hours in the kitchen with all of us gathered around and watching. As he cooked, he described the benefits and the practicality of his pots and pans. He gave us dozens of reasons why we should use them in our kitchens. But the rough way he handled the cookware and his obviously memorized sales talk didn't ring "true." He didn't convince any of us to buy.

After our guests had gone, my husband and I had a last cup of coffee with the salesman, and he began to confide in us. He said that he wasn't selling many sets. In fact, if he didn't make several sales before the end of the month, the company was going to let him go.

I asked him if his wife liked the cookware, thinking, perhaps, she could give him some sales pointers that would help his demonstration.

"Oh, we don't own any. It's too expensive," he said. "We get along fine with our old set."

He had been trying to sell us something he wasn't sold on himself. No wonder his sales pitch was unconvincing. It was only talk, and the customers could sense it.

Using the Word of God in a Bible study is a demonstration of God and His ways. As we study, it will teach us the truth and reality of Christian living. As leaders and guides, we are "sales people," and we should be convinced our product is worthwhile and reliable.

Can You Give Away Something You Don't Have?

It was in a home Bible study that I first heard that salvation was through faith in Jesus Christ, and that we are each responsible to make that decision for Jesus. It was study of the Bible that showed me how far away from God I was.

And so, at thirty-nine years of age, I became a Christian. I was so excited about my new life, I wanted to tell everyone. But how should I tell them? It would be terrible to scare them away with my enthusiasm. Should I say, "Do you know Jesus?" No, they wouldn't understand what I meant. How about, "Are you a Christian?" No, that wouldn't work either. Most of the people I knew were just as I had been. They had gone to church off and on for years and thought they were Christians. After all, as the reasoning goes, if you are not a Jew, aren't you a Christian?

How To Get It

There are all sorts of tools and recipes to bring people to a saving faith, but they all have the same elements:

1. Repentance—which means to repent. You must stop in your tracks and turn around. You need to be sorry for the way you have lived and head toward God. "Repent then and turn to God, so that your sins may be wiped out" (Acts 3:19, NEB).
2. Faith—you need to believe or want to believe that Jesus Christ is God's Son, that he died for your sins, and that He rose from the dead. He's not dead but alive, and He wants to become part of your life. ". . . Believe on the Lord Jesus Christ, and thou shalt be saved, and thy house" (Acts 16:31, KJV).
3. Receiving—you must decide to invite Christ in, and then you actually talk to Him, invite Him to enter your life and help you become the person He has planned you to be. "But as many as received Him, to them gave He power to become the sons of God, even to them that believe on His name" (John 1:12, KJV).

Then, thank Him!

If you have never done this, why don't you take a minute now and do it before you go on with the book.

Now is the time to get to know Him. A wonderful Book has been written that will give you all the details of Jesus' life: Where He was born, where He lived, who He knew, and what He did. You can find out where He is now and what He's doing. God's instructions will help you live your life with a minimum of wear and tear.

CHAPTER 2

Populating Your Study Group

Dick leaned against the pop machine and listened to his co-workers' coffee break conversations, the usual complaints about nagging wives, ungrateful kids, bills, and the heavy responsibilities of being a husband and father.

"Any of you guys interested in finding some answers to our problems?" Dick asked.

"How about divorce?" Jerry said with a laugh. Jerry was a recently divorced man with three small children.

"Hey! How about suicide?" joked another.

"Hey guys, he's serious!" someone exclaimed. The other men looked at Dick with curiosity.

"Sure, I'd like some answers. You got any, Dick?" someone else asked.

Greatly encouraged, he smiled. "No! I haven't. But the Bible does. God has a lot to say. How about getting together Wednesday night at my house and checking it out? Call me if any of you are interested."

That night about nine, Jerry called. He sounded embarrassed. "I'm not sure God has any interest in me or my problems, but if He does, I'd like to find out. Count me in."

A few minutes later another man from work called. "I'm not really interested in Bible study. Wednesday's my poker night. But I've had some tough breaks lately. I don't want to stay home, so I'll just come over and see what's up. But don't sign me up or anything. It's just this once."

It wasn't long before this threesome had grown into a group of nine interested young men enthusiastic about God. They found out together that the Bible has workable solutions.

Why Study the Bible?

There are many reasons people want to be in a home Bible study:

to study the Bible and learn about God.
to find answers to life's problems.
to study biblical history.
to make new friends.

to become part of something.
to find out if God is real.
to ease their loneliness.
to try something new—they've tried everything else.

How Many People Are Needed To Start?

"For where two or three are gathered in my name, there am I in the midst of them" (Matt. 18:20).

For a new Bible study group, two or three are enough people to start with. The important thing is to *begin*. You don't have to wait until you have a room full of interested people. Jesus wants us to use what we have. He will give the increase. The natural result of a spiritual group is growth.

Don't be concerned about the "numbers game." In Bible study it's the individual that counts. Give the few that come the same attention and care that you would give to a much larger group.

Where Are Potential Group Members?

Your Church

With your pastor's approval, use the church bulletin or newsletter to extend an invitation for others to join the study.

Jill wanted to work with new Christians. She asked her pastor if he knew anyone who might be interested.

He hurriedly wrote out a list of twenty-five names of people who had recently accepted Christ through the church's evangelism program. The pastor and others involved in this ministry had not been able to get these new converts together for a follow-up Bible study.

Jill decided to invite eight people to her study. This was to be her first experience as leader, and she wanted a small group.

Armed with this long list of prospective students, Jill sat down and began telephoning. Although she expected to be turned down, the first eight people all said "yes."

Jill was disturbed. If all the people she called were interested, what about the others? They would miss out. With her pastor's recommendation and approval, she called a couple of friends and told them of the situation. They both were willing to help and began calling and inviting the others on the list. Nearly everyone agreed to come.

The three friends offered the identical Bible study in morning, afternoon, and evening sessions. The participants were able to attend any group that was convenient for them.

Jill found it was easy to lead a group with members who had never been in a Bible study before.

They had no idea it was her first time as leader, and they learned together.

Your Friends

When you decide to start a study you will usually remember one or two friends who have expressed an interest in getting together. Perhaps you have common interests or needs: family, marriage, overeating, prayer, etc.

Instead of getting together to "fritter away the time," make it a worthwhile couple of hours. Dig for buried treasure in the Bible.

Your Apartment Building

Cindy, a single gal, wanted to make new friends. She found a Bible study book for "singles." She was interested in using the study, but she had no one to share it with. Living in a large apartment building offered her little opportunity to get acquainted with her neighbors.

She typed up two notices on three-by-five inch recipe cards and put one by the mailboxes in the front entrance and the other in the laundry room. For her own safety she didn't want to put her name or apartment number on the notice. This is how she did it.

ARE YOU INTERESTED IN A BIBLE STUDY FOR SINGLE ADULTS? IT'S A SIX-WEEK STUDY. IT WILL MEET WEEKLY ON MONDAY EVENINGS FROM 7:30 TO 9:00. IT

WILL START MARCH 3 . . . COST $1.50 FOR THE STUDY MATERIAL. PLEASE CALL 892-6600 FOR MORE INFORMATION.

After putting up the notice, Cindy answered the calls by repeating her telephone number in a very businesslike voice. If it was a "crank" call, the caller immediately got the impression he had called an answering service. If the caller was sincerely interested in Bible study, it was obvious by the questions asked and the interest expressed. If Cindy was in doubt as to the caller's intentions, she asked him for his name and telephone number, saying that someone would call him back with more information. Honest individuals did not hesitate to give her the information. Others hung up or gave phony names and addresses. With no other identification than her telephone number on the notice, the possibility of the wrong people getting her name and apartment number was practically eliminated. Also, it was impossible for anyone to simply "drop in" the day of the study. Cindy was able to get a group started that went on to study many different topics together.

Where You Shop

There are usually bulletin boards in grocery stores and laundromats. Use Cindy's method.

Your Neighborhood

Have an informal get-together to discuss the

possibility of forming a Bible study group. Hold the meeting during the same hours you intend to have the study. Some suggested times:

Morning 9:30 A.M.
Afternoon 1:30 P.M.
Evening 7:30 P.M.

If you know the people, invite them by telephone. If you aren't acquainted or prefer to send an invitation, type or write a simple one and mail it or drop it off at their homes. The invitation should be light-sounding, but informative. Don't get people to your meeting under false pretenses. Be sure to say the meeting is an "informational coffee." Sample Invitation:

Dear ________ ,

You are invited to an "informational coffee" to get acquainted with others in the neighborhood and discuss the possibility of forming a Bible study group.

WHERE:	13949 Pleasant Lane
DATE:	Monday, January 17, 19___
TIME:	9:30 A.M.

Sincerely,

Alice Jimu
849-5822

The Informational Coffee

Caution: Your informative coffee hour should not be "religious." Don't open with prayer or use Christian terminology, such as "God spoke to my heart and told me to have a study," or "I've been led to start a group" or "What a blessing it will be to feed on God's word." These words may be familiar to you and a part of your vocabulary, but they will be a foreign language to many.

Don't scare people away. Draw them in. Have name-tags available, but don't insist that they be used. To some people name-tags are threatening. They tend to make some people feel they have already "joined" and are now a part of the group.

What To Serve at the Informational Coffee

Serve a beverage suitable to the weather: coffee, tea, hot chocolate, punch, hot or cold apple cider. At an evening meeting offer a decaffinated beverage. Always have ice water available for those who want it.

The food item should be something simple, and not sticky or crumbly. Remember, many people are dieting—don't tempt them. A bread is always a good choice. You can choose from pumpkin, date, or banana. They are moist, yet easy to eat.

How To Serve

Buffet style is easy, practical, and casual. All

help themselves as they come into the meeting. Have the food and beverage easily obtainable. Set your table neatly and cleanly—nothing elaborate. This is not the time to show off the family silver. Don't forget the napkins, sugar, cream, spoons, forks, and ashtrays.

Explaining the Study

After refreshments, thank the people for coming and tell them it was good to get to meet them. Explain that you are interested in helping form a Bible study group and extend an invitation to them to join.

People cannot commit themselves to something they don't understand. They want to know what they are agreeing to. Anticipate their questions and provide the following information:

1. The study will usually meet once a week at the same time and place.
2. There will be a short time of visiting and then the study.
3. The study will last from one to two hours (each groups decides this).
4. The material you intend to study. (If you have not picked out material, tell them that the group will decide later what it will study.)
5. The possible cost of the study material.
6. The length of the study. If you choose an eight-week study, plan on nine weeks, using the

first week to hand out material, acquaint them with the study, and, perhaps, to work the first study together.

Explain that the study is interdenominational—everyone is welcome. Tell them the study is based on the Bible and not affiliated with a church. The nature of this study will not offend anyone's denominational feelings but will supplement them.

Ask the people to consider being part of this group and give them a week or two to decide. Suggest that they call you *if they are interested.* This way those who are not will not have to call and offer an excuse.

Don't feel hurt if everyone isn't as excited over a Bible study as you are. Not all the people attending the coffee will join the study. Be gracious, loving, and kind to everyone. Give them the freedom to make their own decision without feeling guilty.

CHAPTER 3

Choosing the "Right" Materials

Choosing Bible study materials is like buying a new pair of shoes. After you notice you need them, you begin to shop around to see what's available. Most of us have a certain amount we can spend, and we want to get the best we can for the money. We want our shoes to look good and feel comfortable. Often we buy footwear for a special occasion—we wouldn't wear golf shoes to a wedding. The same general principles are true in choosing Bible study materials to "fit" a particular group.

Shoes That Fit

Here's what to look for when selecting materials:

1. A study book that meets the needs of the majority of the group.

2. One that everyone can afford. Each person needs her own if she is to get the maximum benefit. It's against the law to make copies of material that is copyrighted.

3. Do you like the study? Do you understand it?

4. Is the gospel presented? Will each person get a chance to accept Christ?

5. Does it require the participants to study the Bible to find answers for the study questions?

The Wrong Size

Here's what to avoid in picking a study:

1. Studies that are too long to complete a lesson each session.

2. Studies on the book of Revelation. Our natural curiosity wants to explore the mysteries in Revelation, but the symbolism is too complex for the novice to understand.

3. Materials that push what the author thinks instead of what the Bible says. Beware of people who "ride hobby horses." We can get into error by adopting a teacher as our ideal and studying the Word through his or her insights and beliefs.

4. Studies that do not relate the Bible to today and our modern problems.

5. Lessons that focus on denominational dis-

tinctions rather than on the commonly accepted truths of Scripture. These studies tend to divide rather than unite.

Narrow Your Choice To Three

Here are some tips for making your final choice:

1. *Think!* Start by using your mind. What kind of a group do you have or want to have? Couples? Young people? Housewives? Businessmen? Visit a Christian bookstore and look over the studies in the different categories, or use the list that is provided in this chapter. Narrow your choice to three studies that you believe will meet the needs.
2. *Vote!* If you are choosing the study *as a group,* bring the three books or the information about them to the group for them to look over and consider. Let them decide by vote which to use. Some Christian bookstores will let you take a few books home on consignment to help you make up your mind.
3. If you are choosing the study *for the group,* again narrow the choices down to three.
4. *Pray!* Tell God that you want to lead the study He wants. Ask Him to reveal His will to you.

If any of you lacks wisdom, let him ask God who gives to all men generously and without reproaching, and it will be given him (James 1:5).

Then don't just sit there waiting for God to speak and tell you which of the three to use. Just go back to your normal, daily routine. As you go about your business, you will begin to think more about one of the studies than the others. It may take several days, a week, or even longer, but you will have an ever growing certainty about which study you should use. God will let you know.

But the wisdom from above is first pure, then peaceable, gentle, open to reason, full of mercy and good fruits, without uncertainty or insincerity (James 3:17).

To me this means I can be sure I've made the right decision.

How To Know the Group's Needs

Whenever we build anything, we first need a good foundation. Start with a basic beginner's Bible study. After you work a few weeks on this study, you will have a better idea of the needs of the group.

If You Already Have a Topic

Paul wanted to lead a study on fasting. He valued fasting and knew it was important for believers to understand and practice. He mentioned his idea to a few friends. They all wanted to be in a study group, but each had a different topic suggestion. Paul became confused. Instead of studying fasting, he allowed his friends to choose something else. Since he had no "feeling" for the study, he neglected to do his homework. The others sensed his lack of interest, and their enthusiasm flagged also. Paul was trying to please his friends and didn't take a firm lead. Their time spent together was disorganized, and it became a "study" without study. The group didn't grow, people stopped coming, and finally it died.

If you have a special love for a topic or subject and you feel you are to lead, use your topic. God will draw others to the group with the same interest and need.

Making Your selection

Here is a list of recommended study books. Each entry shows the author, publisher, price (at the time of this writing), number of weeks the study lasts, and a brief description of the contents.

Obviously, this list does not include all of the Bible study books available. These are just examples of guides I have used or am acquainted with. Your pastor, priest, or elder can advise you on the reliability of materials not listed here.

The list is divided into categories to help you identify the best study for your particular group.

Contact your local bookstore to order the material. If the study you choose is not in stock, the bookstore will order it for you.

Basic Beginning Bible Studies

These studies are designed to bring people to a saving faith and get them going for God. They are appropriate for men, women, couples, singles, and teens.

1. *How To Live Forever,* by John Phillips.

For nonbelievers; blanks to fill in—answers included; eight weeks; Moody Press; study $1.25.

2. *Basic Bible Study For New Christians,* by Keith L. Brooks.

Blanks to fill in; leader's guide with answers; eight weeks; Moody Press; study $1.25; leader's guide $1.25.

3. "Lessons" series

Lessons on Assurance
For brand new Christians; questions to answer; five weeks; Navpress; study $0.30.
Lessons on Christian Living
Questions to answer; eight weeks; Navpress; study $0.35.

4. "Love" series; all by Richard Peace; can be ordered separately; five weeks each; Zondervan; study $1.25.

Learning to Love God
Blanks to fill in.
Learning to Love Ourselves
Blanks to fill in.
Learning to Love People
Blanks to fill in.

5. *Studies In Discipleship*

To help you become a real follower of Jesus Christ; seven weeks; for information on ordering, write to Grason, Box 1240, Minneapolis, Minnesota 55440; please allow 4 weeks to get the material (it's worth waiting for); study $0.75.

Studies For Believers or Interested Nonbelievers

6. *Can You Run Away From God?* (Jonah), by James Montgomery Boice.

Discussion questions at end of each chapter; five weeks; Victor Books; study $1.50; leader's guide $0.75.

7. *Faith In Action* (James), by Chuck and Winnie Christenson.

Blanks to fill in; basic leader's guide included; ten weeks; Harold Shaw Publishers; study $1.45.

8. *Letters to Two Young Men,* by Calvin W. Becker.

Using 1 and 2 Timothy and Titus; blanks to fill in; basic leader's guide included with answers; eight weeks; Moody Press; study $1.25.

Studies For Believers Only

9. *Keys To Triumphant Living* (2 Corinthians), by Edgar C. James.

Blanks to fill in; leader's guide with answers included; twelve weeks; Moody Press; study $1.25.

10. *Building Up One Another,* by Gene A. Getz.

Discussion questions included; leader's guide in book; interesting and practical; twelve weeks; Victor Books; study $2.25.

11. *What Works When Life Doesn't?* by Stuart Briscoe.

Practical help from the Psalms; leader's guide

has Victor multi-use transparency masters; challenging; twelve weeks; Victor Books; study $1.95; leader's guide $1.95.

12. *Disciples Are Made,* by Walter Henricksen.

Discussion questions; challenging; advanced; twelve weeks; Victor Books; study $1.95; leader's guide $0.95.

Studies For Men Only

13. *The Godly Man,* by Gene Warr.

For believers; blanks to fill in; twenty-two weeks; Creative Resources; study $2.95.

Studies For Young People

14. *Jesus and Me,* by Gladys Seashore.

For believers and nonbelievers; blanks to fill in; twelve weeks; His International Service; study $1.50.

Studies For Couples

15. *A Handbook For Engaged Couples,* by Robert and Alice Fryling.

For believers; questions to fill in; no nonsense!;

intense and revealing; fifteen weeks; InterVarsity Press; study $2.95; leader's guide $1.95.

16. *Two Become One,* by J. Allan Peterson.

Marriage and family; blanks to fill in; no leader's guide; for believers; thirteen weeks; Tyndale; study $2.95.

Studies On the Family

17. *Building Your House On The Lord,* by Steve and Dee Brestin.

On marriage and parenthood; blanks to fill in; leader's guide included; fifteen weeks; Harold Shaw Publishers; study $1.45.

Studies For Women Who Enjoy Crafts

18. *Consider Christ,* by Daisy Hepburn.

Involves work and creativity for leaders and students; easy, imaginative, and fun; believers or nonbelievers; seven weeks; Victor Books; study $1.50; craft ideas/leader's guide $0.50.

19. *Some-One Special,* by Gladys Seashore.

Crafts and poetry; interesting for all; for believers as well as nonbelievers; ten, forty-minute lessons or five, one-and-one-half hour sessions; His International Service; study $1.00.

Basic Studies For Women

20. *The New Me*, by Gladys Seashore.

For believers or nonbelievers; blanks to fill in; each week has a topic: marriage, family, etc.; questions to answer; no leader's guide; nine weeks; His International Service; study $1.50.

Studies For Women Believers

21. *You Can Be The Wife Of A Happy Husband*, by Darien B. Cooper.

Marital success; thirteen weeks; Victor Books; study $2.50.

22. *Coping With Life And Its Problems*, by Joyce Marie Smith.

Basic leader's guide included; blanks to fill in; twelve weeks; Tyndale Publishers; study $1.75.

23. *A Woman's Priorities*, by Joyce Marie Smith.

Studies of women of the Bible; blanks to fill in; basic leader's guide included; twelve weeks; Tyndale Publishers; study $1.25.

24. *Lord Change Me,* by Evelyn Christenson.

On becoming the person you want to be; for the advanced student and leader; challenging; has visual aids; thirteen weeks; Victor Books; study $2.95; leader's guide $1.95.

CHAPTER 4

Leading—There's More Than One Way

How does a leader lead? Sorry, I can't tell you precisely what methods to use or how to be certain the lessons are absorbed. You'll have to find what works best for you.

Preparation

Most Bible study books have a leader's section with instructions on how to work with the class. Others have separate "leader's guides," which include detailed instructions telling the leader exactly what to do.

When I'm preparing to lead a lesson, I try to find a quiet place to study. During the years when our three daughters were teen-agers and living at home, the only "quiet" was between 11:00 P.M. and 6:00 A.M. I formed the habit of getting up after everyone else was asleep to work undisturbed.

Now, with my Bible study book, leader's guide (if there is one), pencil, paper, and a pot of tea, I settle in to learn about the Lord and the lesson.

But first, I assemble my reference books. I enjoy working with:

The Bible

Webster's Dictionary

Young's Analytical Concordance (Grand Rapids: Eerdmans, 1975).

The New Compact Bible Dictionary (Grand Rapids: Zondervan, 1967).

What the Old Testament Is All About, by Henrietta Mears (Glendale, Calif.: Gospel Light Regal Books, 1977).

A Look At The New Testament, by Henrietta Mears (Glendale, Calif.: Gospel Light Regal Books, 1966).

Insights into Bible Times and Customs, by G. Christian Weiss (Lincoln, Neb.: Back to the Bible Broadcast, 1972).

The Way It Was in Bible Times, by Merrill T. Gilbertson (Minneapolis: Augsburg, 1959).

If I am just starting a new study book, I briefly skim through the entire book and the leader's guide for an overview.

Next I go through the lesson carefully, looking up any additional suggested Scriptures. I try to find the geographical location of the places mentioned in the verses listed and read anything in my reference books that will help me understand the times, people, and places of the lesson.

I look up any words that might not be clear or understood by group members and write the meanings in the margin of my study book or teacher's guide. For instance, in the book of James we find the word *wisdom*. Webster's dictionary says wisdom is: "good judgment and prudence." I looked up "prudence" and it means "careful management." I hadn't been aware before of that meaning. My *Compact Bible Dictionary* says wisdom is "an attribute of God," and it shows many additional biblical meanings of the word.

Finding meanings for words broadens your understanding and gives depth to the study. But be wise. Don't use your whole time with the group discussing words.

I fill out my Bible study book as if someone else were leading the study. I don't think about teaching others at this point. I'm learning for "me." Often I reread a question to be sure I understand it. Sometimes my first response to a question is a "shallow" one. I work to find a better, deeper answer.

Then I make notes on any questions the study brings to mind. Usually others will have the same thoughts. For example, John's baptism, as referred to in Luke and John, implies there is more than one type of baptism. I would look in my Bible dictionary under "baptism" and find out all I could in case anyone was confused. When leading the study I wouldn't draw attention to it, but I would be prepared in case someone questioned it.

Don't Get Lazy

I have a favorite study for new believers and have used it many times. The second time I gave it I was sloppy in my preparation and study because I thought "I knew it." When we got into it, I was amazed. It seemed like a new study. There were so many fresh insights to the same material. Now I know I can't presume upon previous knowledge but must go over each lesson as if for the first time.

Each of us is unique—God will help you find what *you* should do to be effective.

But we all have one thing in common. We each have to teach for the "first time." Leading, teaching, guiding—or whatever you prefer to call it—becomes easier with practice. The important thing is to begin.

The greatest plus on your side is that when you give yourself to teaching God's Word, within you is the greatest teacher available—the Holy Spirit.

When the Spirit of truth comes, he will guide you into all the truth; for he will not speak on his own authority, but whatever he hears he will speak, and he will declare to you the things that are to come. He will glorify me, for he will take what is mine and declare it to you (John 16:13,14).

But the Counselor, the Holy Spirit, whom the Father will send in my name, he will teach you all things, and bring to your remembrance all that I have said to you (John 14:26).

The Typical Leader/Guide Method

The dictionary says that to "teach" means to show how to do something . . . to train, give lessons to . . . instruct, to provide with knowledge. And "lead" is defined as to direct, as by going before or along with, to direct by influence, to show the way.

A leader working alone usually decides on the meeting place—sometimes its her own home. She makes the refreshments or asks someone else to help. She has the responsibility of leading the study, which includes keeping the group on the subject and moving the study along. She assigns lessons and works to draw out the truths from the Scripture.

The leader can also delegate leadership to anyone in the group who she feels can handle it and is willing. Sometimes the leader's guide is passed around, and each person who wants to lead takes a turn.

It is extremely important that any person who offers to be a Bible study leader be under the authority of a pastor, priest, elder, etc. By this, I mean the leader should have the affirmation and approval of a person having spiritual authority. If he gives his affirmation and approval, he should also be willing to help when needed.

The Leader/Hostess Method

In this method:

The leader leads and guides the Bible study.

The hostess offers her home for the meetings and practices the gift of hospitality.

The hostess sees to the comfort of those attending. She opens her home and provides a clean, quiet place for the study. If married, it is important for her to have her husband's approval. She takes the responsibility of keeping an updated list of names, addresses, and phone numbers so that she can call each group member if she needs to cancel a meeting, find out why someone hasn't come, or pass along some other message.

The hostess will probably be more sensitive to the needs of the group than the teacher. She will try to be alert to anyone who needs that extra bit of conversation and encouragement, and she may want to contact this person during the week by phone. She can also on occasion invite several or all of the group members to stay for lunch. This gives an added time of relaxed conversation outside of the structured study. Often at these meals needs are shared and problems solved that are never discussed during the large group meeting.

Being a hostess is more than having a clean house once a week and fresh coffee in the pot. It's an opportunity to minister love and care to those whom God sends. She should be a "warm" person who knows how to make people feel "at home." She should not be so fussy about her house that people feel ill at ease. She must be a kind person, able to talk to strangers and make them feel welcome.

Gail is great as a hostess. She boards horses on her farm and has many chores to do before we arrive on Wednesday mornings. She gets up extra early on those days, but by the time we get there, she is fresh, though perhaps a little breathless. Her face is lit with a beautiful, welcoming smile. She has encouraged us to walk in when we come, not to ring the bell, and to help ourselves to coffee and find a place to sit.

During the meeting, if someone shivers, she brings them a cozy, homemade comforter to keep them warm. She adjusts the heat, opens or closes the blinds—does whatever she can to make the women more comfortable. She watches for these things because she has a servant's heart. She gives us her best and makes us all feel special. Gail keeps extra boxes of tissue in her bathroom and on the coffee table in case someone gets "weepy." People feel at home. Any guest we bring is welcomed as a friend and is encouraged to come back to the study.

Team Teaching

This is my favorite method because I enjoy working with someone else. I like to get "feedback" on how the the study went, and it's good to have someone to talk to if any problems arise.

As team teachers you need to respect each other's capabilities and trust each other with the group.

The woman I teach with is one of my dearest friends. We complement each other because our personalities are different. We make a good team because we are honest with each other in our appraisals of the sessions.

In team teaching you:

- can share the teaching responsibilities by alternating study leadership.
- can give more individual attention to the members.
- can look over the lessons together, and if you wish, choose to lead the lessons you feel more qualified to teach.

- back each other up with prayer.
- always have a spare leader in case of illness or emergency.
- have someone else to discuss problems with and to help out when a difficult question is raised in a study.
- have a second counselor available if counseling is needed.
- can encourage each other.
- can lovingly critique the sessions and discuss together how you can better meet the needs of the group.
- don't feel the heavy responsibility.
- feel more sure of yourself because of your partner's support.

In our team teaching study our basic schedule is:

Coffee first (no treats):	10 Minutes
Singing and worship:	10 Minutes
Study period:	60 Minutes
Sharing answered prayer:	10 Minutes

The teacher who isn't leading the Bible study can lead the singing and worship. She also has the freedom to add anything that might help during the discussion period. She does try, though, to keep her additions to a minimum, remembering that it isn't her turn to lead.

Also for couples' studies, consider having multiple leaders—two couples who alternate responsibilities.

Don't Forget To Pray

Before you go to the study, have a time alone with God. Tell Him that you need Him to help you do and say the things that will please Him. Ask Him to use you and give you the necessary gifts for this service. Ask Him for wisdom, strength, and love for those in the study. Ask Him to help you recognize those who are hurting so that you can minister to them. Ask Him to fill you with His Holy Spirit, and then believe that He has.

CHAPTER 5

You as the Leader

The buzzing in my ears was getting farther away. The droning noise faded into a gentle hum. Suddenly, my arm slipped out from beneath my head. I jerked and woke up.

My Bible study teacher was standing beside me, looking down at me in a very unpleasant way.

"I'm sorry," I murmured. "Must have been the warm room . . . I was up late last night . . . sorry." I picked up my Bible, notebook, and coat and shuffled out with the others. We were all yawning and grumbling as we left the stuffy room.

I had signed up for a six-week study on biblical history, and I was determined to finish in spite of the boring way the material was being presented. The teacher had a love for the dates and historical facts he continually tossed out to his less than receptive audience. He "loved" to teach. He seemed enthralled with the sound of his voice and his vast knowledge of history. I wouldn't have been surprised if he had given us the exact number of flies hatched in Egypt in A.D. 65.

It was obvious to all, our teacher wasn't aware or concerned about our lack of response and interest. He was satisfied listening to himself.

Leaders should develop an awareness of their group. They need to learn how to *Stop, Look,* and *Listen.*

1. *Stop.* Learn to stop on time. People will "turn you off" when you go beyond the scheduled time. Sometimes it can't be helped; time just gets away from us. But we must realize that people have places to go and things to do.

2. *Look.* As you teach are you getting eye contact from the persons in the group or are they staring off into space? Are they looking at the clock, yawning, or falling asleep? Are they gathering their books and Bibles, getting ready for dismissal? Has anyone put on his coat or edged toward the door? Has anyone left?

3. *Listen.* Is your voice the only one you hear? Have you been hearing it for a long time? When you become wordy, you lose the attention and respect of the class.

I have a tendency to give more information than is necessary, and I have to watch myself. I need to "feed the sheep," but not stuff them so full they have digestion problems.

Study the Fabric

When I began leading Bible studies, I would let a single lesson dribble on for two or more sessions, thinking that it was deeply satisfying to plow through it. I have since learned there is a better way.

First, I read through the lesson myself at home, answer the questions, and observe what I am reading. I ask myself, "What is the lesson teaching?" Then I pray and ask God to draw out the truth of the teaching. As I study I see a direction that He wants me to go—one area that He wants expanded more than the others. Some of the questions are very basic, but together they draw out the deeper truth. They are the threads that make up the fabric. You should observe the fabric—don't study threads.

The people who write studies divide them into chapters for a reason. A chapter in a study book is both a unit of teaching and learning. The questions provided serve to teach the unit. Now I find that if each group member does her lesson at home, she has put the Scriptures into her mind and (I hope) her heart, and the teacher (the Holy Spirit) can draw from that input.

Each lesson will have a main truth, and it shouldn't take weeks to find it.

We Remember What We See

If you are comfortable with a chalkboard, use one to outline the lesson, list suggestions and ideas, define words, make assignments, and review previous lessons.

If a chalkboard is unavailable, newspaper pages (want ad sections work especially well) draped over an easel, or propped up on a breadboard, or tacked on an wall, can be used as a substitute. Use marking pencils to write with.

Or you can make up charts with maps or diagrams, using cardboard and magic markers or felt-tipped pens.

Make Your Questions Clear

Ask one question at a time. The questions should be in a logical sequence so that as the group is answering them, they are learning by building on previous answers.

Address the questions to the whole class. Don't pin anyone down by looking at her when you ask a question, unless you are going around the room in order. If you call on specific people, ask simple questions of those who can't respond to difficult ones. You want each person to feel worthwhile, successful, and capable of making a contribution.

Criticism

As a Bible study leader, you will receive criticism. Some of it will be in love and will be constructive. You and the group will grow because of it. Other criticism will be from a critical or rebellious spirit, which Satan will try to use to bring condemnation and defeat. It is important to realize that in leadership you are vulnerable. Ask for the wisdom of the Lord (James 1:5) and pray that you will be able to discern the spirit of the criticism. If you can learn from it, do so. If it is destructive, forgive and pray for the person who offered it.

Many times a critical person feels inadequate or jealous and has unspoken needs but doesn't know how to ask for help. You will have to learn to put into practice 1 Corinthians 13:4-6:

> Love is patient and kind; love is not jealous or boastful; it is not arrogant or rude. Love does not insist on its own way; it is not irritable or resentful; it does not rejoice at wrong, but rejoices in the right.

Not all criticism is unfounded. I use it as a thermometer to check me out before the Lord. In prayer I bring the criticism to the Lord and ask Him if I need correction. If I do, although it's painful, I receive it. Sometimes I need to make an apology to someone in the group, or restate something I've said, or redo something I've done wrong. I've learned through practice that it's best to make things right immediately instead of waiting.

A criticism can also mean that I've ruffled the waters and the enemy has sent a "fiery dart" to discourage and depress me. When this happens it shows me that I'm doing something positive in the Lord's work, and Satan considers me a threat.

Is It God's Correction or Satan's Condemnation?

God's Way—Light

God's correction always brings light—clear understanding to a problem or situation. God doesn't want to hide things from us if we want to understand. When we pray, asking God for insight, the Holy Spirit will reveal something we have done, said, thought, or taught that wasn't God's will. We will see and there will be understanding and the freedom to ask for forgiveness and a new start—but with understanding of how to do it differently the next time.

Satan's Way—Darkness

When the enemy brings condemnation, he is quick to tell you how stupid you are, or how dumb you sounded and acted. You become depressed. Often you have a general feeling of being "down." You're not sure of what you have done. You can't pinpoint it, but you're sure it must be terrible because you feel rotten, confused, and discouraged. You confess anything and everything you can think of to God, but there's no relief. You don't feel any better, and the depression doesn't go away.

That's not God. God doesn't rub your nose in your sin. He brings you freedom, forgiveness, freshness, and relief.

I have noticed this discouragement sometimes after I've led a Bible study and begun to entertain thoughts of failure. It can really get me down. I've learned to say to God, "Lord, I did the best I could today. If I have failed in any way, forgive me and help me learn from it." Then if the feeling persists, I simply tell Satan, "Get lost!"

CHAPTER 6

Babies and Bibles—Five Answers

Roberta was crying. We had been discussing "the family" in our study group when we noticed her tears. She seldom showed any emotion; she never laughed out loud, acted foolish, or said anything out of place. Nothing seemed to disturb her.

The situation was tense; she began to sob. I moved to her side and put my arm around her.

"What's wrong?" I asked.

"He's gone," she sobbed.

"Who?"

"My husband. He left me last night . . . for a *man*.

I felt sick, but my mind began to search for the right words, and I could hear several of the women begin to pray softly.

At that crucial time, Roberta's energetic four-year-old came running into the room. When she saw her mother crying, she began to sob and scream, "What's wrong with Mommy, what's wrong with Mommy?"

One of the women tried to quiet her and steer her back to the other children playing in the kitchen, but the little girl struggled out of her arms, ran back to her mother, and threw herself in her lap.

Roberta dried her eyes, straightened up, composed herself, and began to console her daughter.

The fragile time of ministry had passed. Roberta withdrew once again into her icy shell. We had had no idea up to that time of the struggles concealed beneath her cold exterior. She never again mentioned her problem.

Children At Studies—Plus or Minus?

Most people arrive at Bible study with worn and tired spirits. They come for a time of refreshing.

Children come to adult Bible studies to see friends, play, and have a good time. They have no desire to be quiet and sit still. It's not their nature. It's an illusion to think they will become spiritual "adults" by osmosis. On the contrary, the continual urging of adults to be still and quiet because the adults are studying the Bible can make them jealous and resentful of the Bible.

A Sad Story

Two Christian friends started a neighborhood study together as hostess and leader. The group began with five persons—three other women and themselves.

The oldest woman, Ella, was in her late forties, edgy and critical. Her husband had deserted her when her teen-age sons were babies. This was her first encounter with Christianity, and since she didn't attend church, it was her only Christian fellowship. She worked nights and came to the morning study at the end of her shift.

Glenda was a worn out, tired mother of six. She lived a life of disappointment and tension in a small, overcrowded house with her husband, children, and a demanding mother-in-law. The hostess's home was a "haven"—neat, clean, and quiet. The tension would leave her face as she settled down in a comfortable chair for the study. For a few hours she was able to put aside her problems and pressures.

Joyce, a recent widow with three small children, was supported by social security and welfare. She was lonely and apprehensive about her future and cried often. She needed special attention.

These three women were beginning to take an active part in the study, preparing the lessons at home and coming eagerly to study God's Word.

They had started to pray simple sentence prayers aloud together and were beginning to open up to each other.

Then Peggy joined the group. Invited at the group's outset, she had missed the first three sessions because of other commitments. She was bright, bubbly, and excited about the study, but when she came with her two preschoolers, problems began. The children were cute, but they were active, noisy, and not well-behaved. This situation often occurs, but the leader and hostess were bewildered and didn't know how to handle it. They didn't want to hurt Peggy's feelings by telling her not to bring the children, but the hostess's home was not equipped for child care and was full of precious items collected over the years. The hostess had to put aside her study to follow the children around, keeping them from getting into things and hurting themselves. The leader hoped Peggy would notice that no one else brought their children to the study; but she didn't, and Peggy didn't seem to be the least aware that they were a disturbance.

Ella was the first to drop out of the study. She said that she needed more sleep.

Joyce cried at nearly every session. Finally, she called the leader and told her Peggy's children were driving her crazy with the noise and constant interruptions. She had tried to ignore it and felt guilty and ashamed of her resentment. She struggled through two more weeks and then stopped coming. They later learned she had joined an evening group.

Glenda became irritable and made some cynical remarks about Peggy's children. Peggy overheard and got angry. They both said some regrettable things.

After this "blow up," the study was full of tension and the women were uncomfortable with each other.

Avoiding the Problem

The subject of children at Bible studies is a delicate one and has to be dealt with carefully. Like everything else, the best way to avoid a bad situation is to handle it *before* it becomes a problem.

A decision should have been made at the initial study and the policy made clear to all. If the members had decided not to have children at the study, it would have been no problem for the leader or the hostess to tell Peggy. Even if she had come the first time with her children, it would not have offended her if the leader would have talked to her privately and told her the policy.

We all learn by experience, but we want the experience to be as painless as possible. The Bible study should be pleasant, peaceful, and profitable for all. Our aim, besides introducing people to

Christ, is to have a group that will foster the growth of love among participants. Often the friends made at a Bible study become lifetime friends.

Five Child Care Methods That Work

But what about the children? Is there a workable answer?

1. *The best solution:* Each woman provides for her own child care.

2. *Find someone who will care for all the children each week.* Check around your neighborhood; ask friends and other Bible study leaders if they know a woman—experienced, loving, and dependable—who would care for your group's children on a weekly basis. Make sure you check her home yourself for cleanliness and safety factors. If possible, get references from others who have used her services. You will be recommending her and are responsible, so don't settle for less than the best.

Find out the following details about your babysitter: address; telephone number; what she charges per child (does she give a discount for more than one child per family?); what door the mothers should use when bringing the children; any other details that would be helpful.

Decide on a time agreeable to the sitter when the mothers can leave and pick up their children. Then, as leader, you must start on time and finish the sessions early enough to allow the women to pick up the children at the specified time.

3. *Use the home of a study participant for "baby-sitting headquarters."* Beth wanted to join a Bible study but was concerned about finding someone to care for her three preschool children. Her husband suggested the study group use their home as a headquarters since it had all the necessary equipment; cribs, play pens, toys, etc.

His idea was an answer to the other mothers' problems too. When Beth joined the group, all of them began to bring their children to her home. The children enjoyed this arrangement. They made friends, became familiar with the home and surroundings, and felt more secure than being taken to a different place each week.

Each mother took her turn staying with the children. This meant missing a lesson about once a month. The hostess decided to record each session on her tape recorder, and she sent it home with Beth for the babysitter, who listened to the tape during the next day or so. The tape was then available to anyone else who might have missed the study.

4. *Exchange child care with another study group.* Find another home Bible study group in your area and arrange to exchange child care with its members. Be sure to share your rules with them so all participants have a complete understanding of what will be expected of them.

5. *Alternate homes.* The mother doing the

baby-sitting uses her own home. The other children are brought to her. It's easy to accommodate a few more children in a home already set up for child care. This method usually involves only a few different homes for a small study group.

If You Must Have Children At The Study . . .

Try to keep the children in a separate part of the home, away from the sound of mother's voice. The mothers can take turns staying with them in a playroom or basement area. If the weather permits, they can be outside.

The problem remains the same: the probability of interruptions. When a child is aware that Mom is near, it's inevitable that he will think of dozens of reasons to see and talk to her. There will be noise coming from the children and the result is disturbance. Someone is going to miss out on something, and the study will "miss its mark."

*Ten Simple Rules for Pleasant, Successful Child Care**

1. If in a private home, have the husband's approval to use the home.
2. Replace any toys or personal belongings your children break.

*Please feel free to copy these rules and hand them out at your first meeting or informational get-together.

3. Furnish your own children's milk, diapers, etc.
4. Don't bring the children earlier than the agreed upon time and pick them up promptly.
5. Keep your children home if they are sick.
6. If there is a charge, bring the right change to pay the sitter. Don't run up a bill.
7. Be willing to take your turn as sitter. If you have to miss your turn, make it up as soon as possible.
8. Give the sitter a telephone number for emergencies.
9. If the children have snacks as a group, take your turn furnishing the food and beverages.
10. If your sitter is a volunteer, help her pick up toys, etc.

Don't expect all the women in the Bible study to volunteer to baby-sit. Ask only the mothers using the service.

Suggest that the mothers make this time each week special for their children. If they are encouraged to enjoy it, they will. If the parents ask questions and show an interest in their activities, the children usually respond enthusiastically and cheerfully.

Baby-Sitting: a Ministry?

"I'm just the baby-sitter." What an understatement! Baby-sitting is one of the greatest ministries available to the "average" Christian woman.

Claudia uses this time with the children to instruct them in the ways of the Lord. She reads them stories, helps them to share and care for each other, and encourages them to put toys away and take care of books and games. At snack time they sing songs of blessing and thank God for what He has provided. She has taught them conversational prayer, and if a child gets bumped, they all gather to pray for the hurt little one.

Claudia doesn't just "sit" by parking herself down to watch the children play. She is involved with them—loving, caring, and guiding.

Some women have a special love for children and have no "outlet." Child care is one way, and a very important way, to serve the Lord and minister love.

Consider offering yourself as a children's teacher (baby-sitter). If it's not necessary that you get paid, offer your services free. You will find that God has many ways of rewarding you.

Baby-Sitting Suggestions

Claudia works with little children and offers this advice:

1. *Use puppets, dolls,* or *stuffed animals* to tell a story.

2. *Use a flannel board*—figures and scenery. For a change, record a story on a cassette tape (your voice) and play it for the children. You will be free to show facial expression and concentrate on changing the flannel board figures and scenery.

3. *Use nature*. Make crafts from common items—rocks, pine cones, walnut shells, little pieces of wood. Try making animals from pompons and felt. Have the projects simple enough so each child will be able to complete them.

4. *Be active*. Children need a physical activity time, too. They love it and will burn off some of that "extra energy." Teach them a marching song, then let your inhibitions go and march with them. A march is an activity that is quite easy to control.

5. *Eat*. Snack time is very important to little children. Teach them to ask the Lord's blessing with a prayer of thanks before eating.

6. *Act*. Find Bible skits or make them up using the Scriptures for the script. Make sure the children know you are acting out real happenings.

7. *Give responsibilities*. Make them feel important and let them learn how to participate by helping. This makes them feel they are a part of the group. Be sure you distribute the jobs evenly—don't overlook the quiet ones or develop "pets."

8. *Be a child*. Get on the floor with them; go down to their level; see what they see. Before you begin explaining something to them, try to remember how they think—what they understand at

their age. They are not "little adults," but children.

Successful Story-Telling

If a group of children is too large for one teacher during story time, divide the group into two or three small groups. Number or name each group. Call the different groups separately to yourself in a quiet part of the room and tell them the story.

Encourage the others to color or play quietly until their group is called over. Tell the same story to each group.

Sometimes the children who are quiet and interested will listen three times. Each child should hear the story at least once.

CHAPTER 7

That All-Important First Meeting

We knocked and waited, hunching our shoulders against the biting November wind that nearly blew us off the steps.

"It's Tuesday the third, isn't it?" I asked my companion.

"Yes! And it's 9:30, too," she said between chattering teeth.

"Isn't anyone home?" I thought of pounding on the door, but I hesitated, wondering if we might have made a mistake. I was cold and getting a little angry.

I dug into my coat pocket and pulled a scrap of paper out. It read . . .

Bible study—Tues., Nov. 3, 9:30 A.M., 16694 Grand Avenue.

"This is right! Something must be . . ."

Just then the door slowly opened and a sleepy face peered out.

"Hi!" I said, "Is the Bible study here today?"

"Oh, yeah! Come on in. . . ."

This was my introduction to Bible study at Elaine's. Every meeting ran the same—at least the ones that I attended. She was never ready; the house was a mess; everyone came late.

I came to study the Bible, but I found myself learning nothing and getting more irritated each week. I finally stopped going. Elaine had volunteered to be the leader and had promised to feed me (spiritually), but I always went home hungry.

Inform the Group Members

Whatever method you have used to form a group—informational meeting, friends, bulletin board, notices, newspaper ads, church—it is important that each person who has expressed an interest be informed of the date, time, and place of the important first meeting. Call or send a notice to everyone.

Set an Example

As a leader, whether you like it or not, you set an example. Always be on time and prepared.

Make it a point to arrive at the meeting place ten

to fifteen minutes before the others. Use this time to set up chairs, blackboard, or tables and arrange any materials you will use. Get comfortable! If the group is small, plan to gather around a kitchen or dining room table. Or, if you use the living room, arrange the seating so that each person will be able to see you and the others.

It's important that you be ready and calm. Set the scene, create an atmosphere; let it be one of "peace."

Pray In Advance

Take a few minutes before the others arrive to invite the Lord to the meeting—you need Him. Ask for His help. My prayer goes something like this:

Dear Lord, thank you for this opportunity to serve You. Fill me with Your Spirit and Your wisdom. Give me Your love for these You send, and Lord, make me sensitive to their needs. Send the Holy Spirit to open our spiritual eyes and ears so we can understand and apply Your Word to our lives. Without You, I can do nothing. Thank You. Amen.

Make It Friendly

The first meeting is an example of what the others will be like, so make it great!

Welcome them! Greet them! Love them! God has sent these people to you. He has drawn them by His Spirit. They want to find out about Him and His Word. They have needs. They're not intruders!

No matter what type of group you have, someone has to be the "greeter." If you are both the teacher and the hostess, you should do it. If you're team teaching, both of you can take this responsibility. If you use the teacher/hostess method, the hostess should be the greeter.

I can still remember vividly the welcome I received at my first Bible study. I was awed by the caring and love I felt from those strangers. That welcome helped bring me back when I wanted to stay away.

Greeter's Duties

The leader of the group will determine by what she wears what the "dress code" will be. If you meet the women at the door in dirty blue jeans and an old flannel shirt, the next week you'll find each lady dressing down to meet your standards. If you meet them in your "party best," they will feel intimidated and inadequate. Try to find a happy medium. Wear comfortable clothing—neat, clean, and fresh. The others will follow suit.

Wear your name tag so they can see right away who you are. Meet everyone with a *smile*. Don't be a "sour apple." Talk! Say "Hello," "Hi," or "Welcome."

If you are a "handshaker," shake hands. If you are a "hugger," *don't.* If it's a new group, your affection might scare some away.

Before I came to know Jesus, I couldn't stand to have anyone touch me, especially another woman. It gave me the "creeps." I found out later that it was I, not the huggers, who had the problem.

Give Them Name Tags

A name tag and a pen to write with are the first order of business. You can fill out the tags yourself or you can steer your guests to a table where they can do it themselves. The name tags can be as fancy or as simple as you want. If you are artistic, you can cut them out in interesting shapes—dove, fish, star, leaf. Or plain rectangles of paper two-by-three inches will do, too. Remember to furnish a straight pin with each tag.

Name tags will encourage those coming first to talk to each other, and they probably will be chatting comfortably before the others arrive.

Coffee, Tea, Goodies

It's up to you. A beverage is a good "ice breaker," but watch the "goodies." Many can't eat sweets, and many shouldn't.

Some groups like to have coffee waiting for the women when they arrive. Lately, I've noticed most hostesses have a pot of hot water with instant beverages—coffee, tea, hot chocolate—available. That way, nothing but water gets thrown away.

Ash Trays

Have them available for the smokers, and have plenty of ventilation for the nonsmokers.

Start On Time

Don't wait for latecomers. This first meeting will determine the pattern for the others, and it is important for the group to know sessions will begin at the scheduled time.

Pray With the Group

An opening prayer will settle the group and signal that the meeting is now beginning. Don't be "wordy" or try to impress anyone with your prayer. Remember, you are talking to God. A sample prayer:

Dear Lord, thank You for each person here. We invite You to be with us and help us in our study and our decisions. In Jesus' name, amen.

Get Acquainted

Introduce the leader (or leaders) and hostess. Play a simple get-acquainted game. There are many games like this, but this is the one I use.

> Start with the leader. Go around the group one by one. Say your name, a hobby, and your favorite food.
>
> Leader: "My name is Norma Spande. I like to sew and my favorite food is pizza."
>
> The next person: "Her name is Norma Spande. She likes to sew and her favorite food is pizza. My name is Myrl Seledic. I like crafts and my favorite food is lobster."
>
> The next woman: (She looks at me first.) "Her name is Norma Spande. She likes to sew and her favorite food is pizza." (Looking at Myrl) "Her name is Myrl Seledic. She likes crafts and her favorite food is lobster. My name is Nancy Ernewein. I like to bowl and my favorite food is chicken Kiev."
>
> And on and on around the room until each person has taken her turn. No one wants to be last, because they have to repeat all the names and information. It's a little silly, but fun. And it helps strangers to learn others' names and something personal about them.
>
> If you have a large group, use first names only.

Did you notice that we didn't bring up church background or any information on social status? This was done on purpose. You don't want anyone to feel out of place or different. The goal is always to unite, not to divide.

List Names and Telephone Numbers

Ask each person to list her name and telephone number. Sometime a meeting might have to be cancelled, and you will need to be able to reach everyone. Those in charge of the study should have a current list of members for this purpose. Give each person the telephone number of the leader or hostess and the telephone number of the meeting place so that group members can be reached in an emergency.

Record Decisions

Give a sheet of paper to each woman and when the group reaches a decision on how the group will be conducted—announce it. Be sure all have heard and understand, and write it down. This way each will have a reminder to bring home with her.

Miscellaneous Information

The leader or the hostess should give the group any information that will make their time together more comfortable. This will include the location of the bathroom, if there is a special place to park cars, etc.

What Day Will You Meet?

As leader, I usually have only a couple of days when I'm available, and I ask the ladies to choose between these two. If it's obvious that neither of the days I offer will work for the majority, I try to change my plans accordingly. But I do this only after we have exhausted all the possibilities of my offer.

You may find at this point in your discussion that one or two of the people will not be able to attend on the day and time agreed upon. It is almost impossible to please everyone. Usually, if a person is interested in attending a Bible study, she will have to make some adjustments in her schedule. Setting up priorities is an important part of our spiritual growth. You might find that some want God but not enough to alter their personal schedules.

What Time Will You Meet?

The times listed below are the most common time frames for studies:

9–11:30 A.M.
1–2:30 P.M.
7–9:30 P.M.

Choose the time that meets the needs of the group. If necessary, feel free to alter your time schedule, by mutual agreement, after you get into the study.

Often study guidebooks suggest limiting your time to one hour. I find it nearly impossible to get acquainted, study, and discuss in just one hour. An hour and a half is more workable for me.

On occasion you will finish before your allotted time is up. Don't drag out a session just to use up the time. Dismiss the group early. It's a refreshing change.

As a leader, it's up to you to stay within the time schedule. Learn to be a good planner and organizer. It takes discipline, but it will be appreciated by everyone.

Working people seem to get left out when it comes to Bible studies. In our area there are very few evening groups. If you have a study at night, be sure to close it off no later than 9:30 P.M. If you go later than that, attention begins to wander and people might fall asleep. Long sessions tend not to build us spiritually; we want to enjoy being together, not become tired of it.

Try to end your meetings when all are having a good time. If you close while you're having fun, everyone will want to come back.

It's much better to hear little cries of, "Oh, no! Is our time up?" rather than, "Finally, we can go home!"

Where Will You Meet?

If you meet in the same place each week, it eliminates confusion. No one will have doubts about where the meeting will be. The participants' families will know where to reach them, and the group will feel established.

As a leader, you have the responsibility of securing the meeting place. You could use your home, the hostess's home, or the home of one of the women in the study. A good rule to follow is that anyone offering her home for meetings must have the approval of her husband.

A Hair Raising Experience

I settled myself down in a comfortable chair and selected coffee and a roll from the tray as it was passed. As I lifted my cup toward my mouth I noticed lipstick on the rim. It wasn't mine. Putting the cup down I picked up my sweet roll and took a bite. You guessed it! My bite was attached to the rest of the roll by a long strand of black hair. I can't stand hair on or in anything except heads, where it belongs. Ugh! I put the roll aside and covered it with my napkin.

The study was excellent. We got into a lively discussion, and the leader was able to get everyone involved.

As I was leaving I glanced down at my black wool slacks. They were covered with hair. It was from either a dog or cat, I wasn't sure which. Now, I love dogs and I like cats, but I don't like their hair on my clothes.

Maybe these things wouldn't upset you, but they bother me. I don't enjoy going to a home that isn't clean and well-kept.

Be careful when you use a home for Bible study. It doesn't have to be fancy, but it should be neat and clean, dusted and vacuumed.

Why You Should Meet Frequently

It's best to meet weekly. It's important in Bible studies to have continual fellowship. You want to get to know each other and become friends. This happens faster when you are together on a weekly basis.

In one of my studies, Liz, a busy executive, always left early, before the others. She would hurry off right after the last question was discussed. She missed out on the conversational prayer, and the small talk that drew the women together. The others in the group became close friends and still see each other now that the study is over. They never got to know Liz.

If You Have Already Selected the Study . . .

Have the books or materials with you at this first

meeting and hand them out. Tell the cost of the books and explain that group members can pay you when they are able. (See further dicussion in this chapter under Money Matters.)

Choosing the Study: the Majority Rules

To eliminate confusion, it's best if the leader narrows the choice to three different study books.

Show the group the three books you have chosen, or if you are using the list provided in Chapter 2, read the titles and tell something about each one. If you have the books with you, read a few chapter headings. Give the group an idea as to the books' contents.

Inform them of the cost and how many weeks they will have to commit to the study (figure one week per chapter).

Pass the books around so they can see them. After a few minutes, vote on which study to use. Of course, majority wins.

Money Matters

Sometimes the leader can charge the books at a bookstore and then be reimbursed by the group members. Often the leader pays for them herself and collects later. It's nice if you can collect from the women before you buy the books, but it usually doesn't work out that way.

After you have decided on a study, collect from the women who have the money and arrange to get the balance from the others at the following meeting. Be sure to write down the names of those who have paid. If you wish you can initial the inside front cover of the study book when they pay you. That way they will have a record of the payment too.

If someone doesn't pay for a book, be willing to absorb this cost yourself. Don't make an issue of it. Often it's a good investment when you provide the Bible study booklets for the group as part of your personal giving.

Buy the Books

Immediately order or buy the books. Distribute them to the people as soon as possible. Deliver them yourself or arrange to have them picked up. Try to get them out so that group participants will be able to complete the lesson at home before the next meeting.

At times you may have a problem getting the books, so when you're selecting your three possible studies from the bookstore, check on their availability. Ask if they have the number of copies you will need in stock. If they haven't, find out how long it will take to get them. If there will be a severe delay, choose another study.

If you won't be able to have the books for the next meeting, I suggest you postpone your study for a week or two until they arrive.

Introduce the Bible

At all meetings have several different versions of the Bible (including a paraphrase), a red letter edition (one where Jesus' words are printed in red ink), and a New Testament. Make sure each person has a Bible. You may need extras to lend out.

If your group includes those unfamiliar with the Bible, have each person find the index. Encourage them to use it until they learn how to find the books of the Bible by memory. Explain the division between the Old and New Testaments.

There may be some in the group who have never held a Bible in their hands and others who have never looked up Scripture. The whole thing looks very complicated, and they may be wondering if they belong. Let them handle the Bible, and as you explain, have them find what you are looking up themselves. Be patient, go slowly, and help them understand that finding verses gets easier with practice.

When I first joined a Bible study, it was a month or more before I realized that the book they gave me to use was a Bible. It had a colorful cover. I thought Bibles were either black or white (with zippers if you were rich!).

The following is a short study on the value of Scripture. Do it with your group. Make it fun and don't hurry.

Using the references listed below teach the group how to pronounce them. Say them aloud. Then together, look them up, one at a time. Take turns reading them aloud. Point out the slight differences between the various versions. Assure them that this is not a problem.

Find and read these passages:

Isaiah 55:1
Matthew 24:35
Hebrews 4:12
John 20:30,31

(With the last passage, explain that there is more than one book entitled John—John, 1 John, 2 John, and 3 John.)

After finding and reading the next verses (below), have individuals paraphrase them (tell them in their own words). Explain that sometimes the study questions will ask you to paraphrase verses from the Bible.

2 Timothy 3:16,17
1 Peter 1:25

How To Do the Lessons

The lessons are to be done at home. The students are to read the assigned chapter and the required Scriptures, and answer the questions. All the Scripture references for a question should be read before the answer is selected.

Assure the group that if they have difficulty answering a question they shouldn't worry about it. Usually, several will find the question difficult, too, and it will open the way for discussion. Urge them to try to write something down (if they use a pencil they can always erase it), and that the whole group will work together to find the appropriate answer.

How the Study Works

Usually go around in a circle, each taking a question and reading an answer. The leader should encourage anyone with more to add to do so, and if there are differences in answers they will be investigated. Explain that because of personalities and interests, it's possible to have different answers and yet not be wrong.

You will have to check each lesson of the Bible study over. There may be more to explain, or another way to approach the Bible study than the way the author suggests. Encourage the group. If you can think back to how you felt at your first Bible study, tell them about it. I'm sure you were once nervous and apprehensive.

Can Others Come?

If you are a new leader, I would encourage you to keep the group to a maximum of eight. If you start with fewer than eight and have room to grow, then invite others up to this number. Take some extra time to go over all the information with each newcomer so they will feel welcome and know what's going on.

Often the studies are continuous and the content builds on preceding lessons. A friend, Myrl, and I team-taught a series and encouraged the women to invite others up to lesson number five. After that, the study was built on the framework of the preceding studies. We had twenty-five women attending and as time passed countless others asked to join. We simply had to say no. It would have been too hard to go back over the previous lessons.

We had to tell the ladies that this was something we had agreed on as leaders and that we would have to uphold that decision. The solution was to tentatively promise we would offer the class again the following year.

Can Children Come?

(Review Chapter 6) The first meeting is the time to set up guidelines for child care. (See my "Ten Simple Rules For Pleasant, Successful Child Care," page 66.)

After leading many Bible studies and working with new Christians, I have come to the conclusion that babies and Bible study don't mix. It's nearly impossible to have a productive time of study and prayer with little children around.

Perhaps some women (usually the mothers) don't mind. But many others do. As leader you must make this decision. Whatever you decide, it's important that you do so at this meeting. Make the decision clear to all.

Commitment

It is very important to get the individuals to agree to commit themselves to the number of weeks it will take to finish the study. Assure them that they are not commiting themselves *forever*, but just for the duration of this particular study.

Dwell on this commitment, how you will depend on each other to contribute to the discussions, attend the meetings, and do the assignments. Remind them that you, as leader, are committing yourself to them, too. Ask them to commit the day and the time each week and give it top priority.

End It Right!

Finally, close with a prayer such as this:

> Dear Lord, thank You for everyone here. Help us commit this study to You that we might make this one of our top priorities for these _______ weeks.
>
> Give us a desire to study Your word and get to know You better. Watch over each one of us until we meet again. In Jesus' name, amen.

Summary Of the First Meeting

You should have:

Been an example, on time, and prepared.
Prayed before the others arrived.
Worn a name tag.
Been friendly, greeted all, introduced yourself and anyone involved in leadership.
Given out name tags.
Served coffee.
Opened the meeting with a brief prayer.
Played a get-acquainted game.
Provided a list of all participants with names and telephone numbers, and given out your name and telephone number.
Given the telephone number of the meeting place so that those attending can be reached if necessary.

Decisions you should have made:

What book you will study.
The number of weeks the study will last.
Where, when, how often the meetings will be held.
Meeting starting and ending times.
Will you have refreshments? What kind?
Will you have children at the study?
Can the members invite others?

They should leave knowing:

A little about the Bible.

How to look up Scripture references.

How to do the lessons, the importance of doing the homework.

The importance of making a commitment to the study and the group.

What decisions were reached.

CHAPTER 8

Partners in Prayer

"Norma," said Peggy, "will you take the responsibility of the opening prayer next week?"

I nearly died. Me? Pray in front of everybody? Out loud? What would I say?

Peggy had really put me on the spot. It was the custom in this Bible study for the women to take turns opening the study with a prayer. But I was the new girl in this group. I really didn't understand what I was doing there or feel that I had the ability to lead in prayer. Yet, more than anything, I wanted to be part of the group and do as the others.

I wondered if there was a book of prayers in the library I could use. Could I find a prayer suitable so they wouldn't know I got it from a book? Another problem I had was that I stammered.

Could I find a prayer with words I could safely say?

I had a whole week. Or rather, *just* a week, to get my prayer together. Each day I worked on it. I didn't want it to be too long, but not too short either. It should sound fairly intelligent, yet not mechanical. What a job! I was nearly sick with worry. I thought about the prayer before I went to bed, while I was trying to go to sleep, and it was on my mind when I woke up. I wrote and rewrote. Finally, I had produced a prayer that would do. Then I tried to memorize it but kept forgetting. I knew I would have to read it.

Bible study morning was a bright and sunny spring day; but my heart was so full of dread I hardly noticed it. When the other women prayed it always looked so simple; I didn't want them to know how afraid I was. I tried to act calm and join in the casual conversation over our coffee before the study. I was so nervous my cheeks felt like cardboard when I smiled. My voice was all "cracky," and I heard myself nervously giggling over unfunny things. I wanted to get it over, yet I hoped they would forget they had asked me. As the time drew closer, the women began to put down their coffee cups and crumple up their napkins. They were ready.

I felt my throat closing. I doubted if I could croak out even one word.

Finally, Peggy said, "Norma, do you have a prayer for us today?"

"Uh huh!" I said, fumbling frantically through my Bible. Panic hit me. Oh, no! What if it had fallen out and I'd lost it. Why didn't I put it in my purse. My face was hot. I felt like crying.

Then I found it. All eyes were on me. It was quiet. All I heard was my breathing and my heart pounding inside of me.

I bowed my head.

> "Dear Father, thank You for loving us. Help us find something today that will help us. Amen."

I could have collapsed after I read it. I almost expected someone to say, "What a nice prayer," or "That was a dumb prayer"; but no one said anything, and we went on with our lesson.

Talking To God—Aloud and Together

Learning to pray aloud in a group is the most frightening, liberating, terrifyingly wonderful thing you, as a Christian, can learn to do. Notice I said *learn.* The only way to learn is by study and practice.

In every study I lead there comes a time when I gently, yet firmly, inform the group that we are all going to pray out loud. After the panic leaves their faces, I explain:

"Let's go around the circle, starting with me, and each of us thank God for something. You can just say one word, one thing you are thankful for." Then, I start. "Dear Lord, we bring to You this morning just one thing out of the many You give us and we thank You for it. Lord, I thank You for my husband." The next person says, "the sunshine," the next may say, "my baby," and so on around the room. When it comes back to me again, I say, "Amen."

This really doesn't frighten anyone. The following week we may do the same thing again, or I might ask them to each name two things they're thankful for. The next week I may suggest that we each thank Him for something we saw in the lesson during the study time.

When they get used to thanking God, then I move them on to asking for forgiveness for one thing they know displeased God. When they can move freely in confessing before the others, then for a few weeks we add prayers of petition.

Then we move into longer conversational prayer where we first thank God for Himself and "things," then confession, then petition. Soon, conversing with God aloud with the others in the group becomes a natural part that is anticipated with joy.

Another Way (For Those Who Have Prayed Aloud Before)

The leader begins by saying, "I praise You, Lord Jesus, because you are my Lord." Someone else says, "living water," and another, "my friend." Each person responds with one phrase at a time as it comes to her. This brings to mind some of the attributes of God.

Vary the ways you start. If you are afraid you are "pushing it," don't go around in order but encourage anyone who wants to join in to just speak out. Those who don't want to pray aloud can pray silently.*

Handling Prayer In Groups

There are nearly as many different ways to handle prayer needs in a group as there are needs. Since there are so many levels of spiritual maturity (some are "old timers" to prayer and study and some are mere "babes"), you alone will have to search and find the ones applicable for your group.

Some leaders like to have their prayer time at the beginning of the session and some prefer it at the end. Experiment and find what works for you. Be flexible. If you see that it cuts into the study, change the prayer time to the end of the session.

Set aside a certain portion of your time together for prayer and set a time limit. Some like to pray and others don't.

You may decide to use a calendar to write spe-

*Reading suggestions: *Prayer: Conversing With God,* by Rosalind Rinker (Grand Rapids: Zondervan, 1959). Also by Rinker, *Conversational Prayer* (Waco, Tex.: Word Books, 1970).

cific time requests to remember when to pray and for how long. Example:

Sue at Bible camp, 7/7-13—that she will accept Christ.

Stop Right Where You Are!

If there is a need expressed that seems to be of an urgent nature, stop and pray then and there for the person or persons. If someone in the group needs counselling and prayer, minister to them during the study if it seems the right thing to do.

Some people always have prayer needs and they want *others* to pray about them. I often suggest to the person bringing forth a need, "Why don't you pray right now and bring your need to God. We will all support you and pray with you silently." This gets them to pray instead of relying solely on the prayers of other people.

Some Problems With Prayer Time

Often too much study time gets used up when each person, one by one, brings forth her problems in lengthy detail. Take the opportunity to teach the women the importance of only sharing the major points with the group.

Leaders must be alert to stop gossip before it harms the study. The guise of wanting someone to pray for a particular problem is often an excuse for a "wagging jaw." This can destroy the study, and the resulting damage to the witness in the neighborhood and Christian community can be permanent.

Instruct your group that there is no need to reveal full names or any other intimate details. The Holy Spirit knows all about the problems, and truly spiritual Christians will avoid prying or passing on confidential details.

Praying Is Talking To God, or Is It?

She bowed her head and said, "Oh, Lord, you know that my brother, the one in Kansas with the bad temper, is coming to visit next week with his wife, Elaine, and their two boys, Tim, 4, and Bob, 6. And you know, Lord, that my husband gets really upset having them around and last time they were here we had a real "blow up," and he said he hoped they'd never come back again. And here they are, coming again. And Lord, they'll have to sleep in our bedroom because we don't have a spare room, and we'll have to sleep downstairs in the musty basement. We sure could use a hide-a-bed, Lord. By the way, Lord, my brother hasn't been working and has written some 'bum' checks. We might have to help them out. . . ."

Who was Lorna talking to? God? Or was she giving a news report to the other women? Remind your group that when they pray they are talking to God, and He already knows the grimy details of their problems.

Pick a Card, Any Card

This prayer request method teaches each person the responsibilities of interceding for another and the joy of being an instrument for answered prayer. It also limits the amount of time spent discussing prayer needs. Usually, only the answers to prayer are shared with the group.

Each person receives a recipe card. Each writes her first name and prayer request. All the cards are placed face down in a convenient place. Sample:

WENDY
~~Wisdom for choosing a new job 4/8~~
My mother will become a Christian
~~A safe trip to Wisconsin 5/12~~
I'll find a Christian friend
at work
~~Our finances will be met in May 5/18~~

At the end of the meeting or when appropriate, each person who has filled out a card and placed it on the pile, draws one. If she draws her own, she puts it back and chooses another.

It is understood that she will intercede for this person and her need(s) during the week between meetings. She is instructed to pray at her regular prayer times and at any other time the Holy Spirit prompts her.

At the next session the cards are returned to their owners. If the prayer has been answered, the card owner crosses out the request and enters the date the prayer was answered. If the prayer has not yet been answered, the request remains on the card for continued prayer.

Recommended reading:

The Kneeling Christian, by an Unknown Christian (Grand Rapids: Zondervan, 1945).

With Christ In The School of Prayer, by Andrew Murray (Old Tappan, N.J.: Fleming H. Revell, 1953).

Helps To Intercession, by Andrew Murray (Fort Washington, Penn.: Christian Literature Crusade, 1970).

You Can Pray as You Ought, by Arnold Prater (Nashville: Thomas Nelson, 1977).

CHAPTER 9

The Bogus, the Biased, and the Beautiful

The Bogus

Last summer a friend of mine opened her house for a Bible study and a stranger came uninvited. She said she had heard there was a study going on and asked if she could join. Since she was so polite and friendly, the leader welcomed her.

The first session went beautifully; the women spent some time getting acquainted and the newcomer was skilled in conversation, interesting, and seemed concerned.

The second week the women were a little disappointed because the new member took over the lead. She used a commentary she brought with her to "clarify" the Scriptures, and she continually referred to her book as the authority.

The third week was a disaster. The stranger dominated the group. She told the women they were "off base" in their interpretations of the Scriptures, and that they needed someone more skilled than their leader to help them see the "truth." She said Jesus was a good man and a mighty prophet, but not the only Son of God. She criticized their denominations and told them they were guilty of keeping pagan holidays.

There were a few new Christians in the study, and they became scared and confused. They wondered if they really were in error.

My friend, the leader, was extremely upset, and headed straight for her pastor to tell him what had happened and to ask for help. The pastor knew right away that this lady was deliberately attending the study to steer the group into false doctrine. He telephoned her that evening, and although he never disclosed the details of their conversation, she did not return.

You shouldn't turn away anyone who is honestly looking for God. But as a leader you have to be aware that your responsibility is to all the women, not just one or two. You have to be able to exhibit control if someone joins the group and brings faulty teaching and doctrine, or tries to usurp the authority of the leader.

To have the backing of a Bible-believing pastor or elder is a must for the Bible study teacher. There are problems that come up that you can't handle. You need a reliable, knowledgeable person you can go to for help.

The Biased

She sat across the room staring at me, eyes ablaze. "You mean to tell me that reading my horoscope is a sin? That's about the dumbest thing I've ever heard. Do you expect me to believe that?"

We were deep into the Book of Acts and reading about the people who brought their books on the magic arts to be burned (see Acts 19). The argumentative lady sat ramrod straight in her chair. She had refused to visit and make friends with the other women. She came late and left early. Not once had she come with her lesson completed as instructed. At every opportunity she broke into the study with something contentious. She continually took personal affront with the Word of God, the study guide, and the other group members. But her real vengeance was saved for the leader—me. She accused me of criticizing her and her way of life. Her statements were prefaced with, "Don't tell me that. . . ." Where do you get that?" "How do you dare tell me?" You mean you expect me to believe that?"

It was discouraging, to put it mildly. She wasn't getting a thing out of the study and was causing trouble and distracting the others. If she would have done her assignments, read the Scriptures, and worked out her lessons, the Bible would have answered her questions and God could have taught her as He was teaching the rest of us. She was a "God Resister."

What did I do? I prayed. I asked God to change her attitude, and I asked Him if there was something wrong in my attitude toward her. I confided in a friend I trusted and asked her for advice and suggestions. We prayed together.

It came to my attention that the woman's sister, who also attended the study, was each week strongly urging this belligerent lady to attend. The day before the study she would telephone her and beg her to try it "just one more time."

I called the sister and asked if this was true. It was. I encouraged the "encourager" to stop encouraging her sister to come!

Was this the right thing to do? All I know is that when she stopped coming, we had peace in the group. It ran smoothly, we enjoyed the time together, and the critical spirit was gone.

There is a time for each person . . . a time when they become spiritually "hungry" for the things of God. Then they want to receive and learn. Forced feeding is not the answer.

The Beautiful

Each week Hannah would sadly report that she hadn't done her lesson. During the discussion she would lean forward and listen intently as the others gave answers to the questions and got into lively dialogue. She always looked so interested I just couldn't understand why she never got around to doing her lesson and reading her Bible. She spoke with a heavy German accent and had some difficulty talking. A few of her words were hard for us to understand.

One afternoon, Alice, a member of the group, telephoned Hannah to say "hello." Hannah invited her over for coffee. While they were visiting, Alice noticed a Bible lying open on the coffee table and, as she picked it up, saw that it was written in German. Hannah blushed and said that it was just her old Bible.

Alice was alert and put two and two together. She asked Hannah if she had trouble reading English. Hannah began to cry and said, "Ja, English is an impossible language." Alice volunteered to come over each week to read the questions to Hannah and help her understand and answer them. Hannah was not rebellious or stubborn, she simply couldn't do her study because of her reading problem. We encouraged her to bring her German Bible to the study.

With some extra effort from a sensitive member of the group, Hannah became able to take part in the study and contribute to the discussions. She also was helped in her efforts to master the reading and writing of English.

Be careful not to judge those in your studies for

their apparent lack of interest or their hasty reactions. Perhaps there is a reason, very personal, like Hannah's, that is keeping them from taking an active part. It's possible they didn't listen or missed the first informational meeting and don't understand what is going on. Maybe they came late and joined the study after it had been going a few weeks. If this is the case, suggest getting together with them to go over the material and tell them the same things you told the others. Show them how to do the lessons. If necessary, work a lesson through with them, especially if they have never been involved in a Bible study before.

Keeping Things "Beautiful"

Newcomers

When someone is new to the group, make a special effort to welcome her and include her in the lesson. Remember, newcomers are important too. Make them feel comfortable, not like intruders. It's easy for a newcomer to get the impression that the others are so far ahead that it's useless to try to catch up.

Take Some Time

Don't be in a hurry to rush off after leading each study. Give the women an opportunity to seek you out to talk with you. Be available.

Personally Contact the "Questioners"

During your studies, watch facial expressions. If you see someone who looks puzzled and might have questions, call her later on the telephone. Comment on the study and tell her you're glad she is a part of the group and ask if she has any questions. You could say, "I noticed you looked puzzled the other day, can I help?" Many people find it easier to talk over the telephone than face to face.

You may want to follow up by inviting the "questioner" to lunch. You can either be alone with her or invite another Christian to be there too. One other person is enough. Any more and she may feel threatened. You can say, "I see that you have a lot of questions; maybe I can help." Or, "You seem to be searching; maybe I have some answers for you."

Prepare To Answer Questions

Anticipate the questions you might be asked in or out of the group. When explaining the gospel, know what to say and when to say it. These books are helpful:

Say It With Love, by Howard G. Hendricks (Wheaton, Ill.: Victor Books, 1972).
You Can Witness With Confidence, by Rosalind Rinker (Grand Rapids: Zondervan, 1962).

If you learn "how to do it," God will give you opportunities to use the knowledge.

You also need to know how to recognize cults and false doctrine. I recommend reading:

The Mind Benders, by Jack Sparks (Nashville: Thomas Nelson, 1977).

So What's The Difference, by Fritz Ridenaur (Glendale, Calif.: Gospel Light Regal Books, 1967).

Have Books and Tracts Available

It's good to have a selection of books and gospel tracts available for group members to borrow. Let them select whatever interests them. These books are part of my portable lending library:

Christy, by Catherine Marshall (Old Tappan, N.J.: Fleming H. Revell, 1967).

Beyond Ourselves, by Catherine Marshall (New York: Avon, 1961).

Prayer: Conversing With God, by Rosalind Rinker (Grand Rapids: Zondervan, 1959).

The Christian Family, by Larry Christenson (Minneapolis: Bethany Fellowship, 1970).

Find Out For Yourself, Eugenia Price (Grand Rapids: Zondervan, 1963).

How To Be Born Again, by Billy Graham (Waco, Tex.: Word Books, 1977).

The Fragrance Of Beauty, by Joyce Landorf (Wheaton, Ill.: Victor Books, 1978).

The Richest Lady In Town, by Joyce Landorf (Grand Rapids: Zondervan, 1973).

The Struggle For Peace, by Henry R. Brandt, Ph.D. (Wheaton, Ill.: Victor Books, 1977).

I'm Out To Change My World, by Ann Kiemel (Nashville: Impact Books, 1974).

How Can I Find You God?, by Marjorie Holmes (New York: Bantam, 1975).

The New Life, by Andrew Murray (Minneapolis: Bethany Fellowship, 1965).

The Christians Secret Of A Happy Life, by Hannah W. Smith (Old Tappan, N.J.: Fleming H. Revell, n.d.).

Tracts/Booklets

My Heart—Christ's Home, by Robert B. Munger (Downers Grove, Ill.: InterVarsity Press, 1954).

Encouraging New Christians, by Michael C. Griffiths (Downers Grove, Ill.: InterVarsity Press, 1964).

Happy Family Life, by Henry R. Brandt & Homer E. Dowdy (Lincoln, Neb.: Back to the Bible Broadcast, 1963).

Some Thoughts On Becoming a Christian

All of us have to start somewhere with God. Not all of us come to know Him in the same way. We have to be tolerant and understanding of the differences in people.

When I first accepted Christ, I thought the way I came to Him was the only way. Only after several years of talking to others and hearing personal testimonies was I able to understand the infinite variety of God's workings. He uses everything to draw people to Him—songs, movies, pain and pleasure, heartache and happiness. We have to be careful we don't put limits on Him.

And, since God knows us best, He knows the unique way to draw us to Him. One of the things that opened my eyes to Jesus Christ was the rock opera "Jesus Christ Superstar," and the song, "He's Just A Man." Now every good Christian knows that "Superstar" is not a Christian play nor Christian music, yet it broke down a barrier in my life, the resistance to Jesus Christ and the truth of His deity.

CHAPTER 10

Danger! Derailment

"I remember when bacon was $0.65 a pound and we could get three pounds of coffee for $1.88."

"And we could get a blouse for $1.99 and a really nice dress for $10."

"I remember when my folks bought a three-bedroom stucco home for $8,000, and it was beautiful."

What is this? Memory lane? A group of economists discussing prices of bygone years?

No! It's a Bible study group—off the track.

Our original subject had been the feeding of the five thousand, and from there we had wandered until we ended up with the price of bacon in 1950.

Someone has to p–u–l–l them back on the track; and as the leader, that someone is you.

Keeping On Track

If someone asks a question that isn't relevant to the study and it interrupts the flow, have a paper and pencil handy and jot it down. Tell the person you will discuss it later with them. Usually, the Lord will answer the question during the study and the person will feel no need to pursue it.

When an interruption occurs you can say something like this:

> "It's important for us to stay on our subject. We'll find that it's very easy to get off on other things. We want to get the most out of our time and our lesson, so when I feel that we have gotten away from our topic, I'll have to bring us back. If I interrupt your conversations, please know it's for that purpose."

Call Out the Stops

Here are a few conversational methods for getting the group back on track:

1. Think of a question pertaining to the lesson; ask it.
2. Remember at what point the discussion got off and say, "We were talking about ________. Let's get back to the point."

3. Repeat the original question if you don't believe it was answered.

4. If it was, say, "Let's go on to the next question."

5. Say, "This is all very interesting, but let's get back to our lesson.

6. Make a cute remark, "Hey! Guys! Come on now, you've lost me."

Sound the Alarm

Sometimes there is so much talking going on that no one is looking at or listening to the leader. Then you might have to resort to violence!

1. Ring a bell.
2. Gently clang your spoon against your cup.
3. Loudly, clap your hands.
4. Whistle.
5. Stand up on your chair and jump up and down.

Whatever you do, *smile* while you are doing it!

Domineering Damsels

Elaine was one of the most dependable women in the study group (she never missed). But she was a "talker," nonstop! She could take any spiritual subject and in two sentences have us so far from the topic that it took a near miracle to get us back.

She seemed to have no interest in spiritual matters, because she would turn every conversation and discussion back to the secular and then talk and talk. If we were patient with her she could use up the whole time with her personal remembrances, dreams, or tales of family situations. We had to interrupt her to get on with the study.

It is very difficult to deal with a person like this, but it has to be done. How do you gracefully interrupt?

Don't Look!

My friend Marj had a great idea. When she told me about it, I could hardly wait for the opportunity to try it. It does work!

When you sense a person has taken hold of the discussion and is not going to "let go," ignore her with your eyes. Don't give her any encouragement by directing your gaze and attention to her. Look at the others or down at your study guide. The others in the group will see that you are not looking at the speaker and giving your "go ahead" for her to continue. They will stop looking at her, too, and begin to give you their attention.

It may take a little time for the speaker to see that you are no longer paying attention, but if she is the least bit sensitive, she will "get the message."

What If They Don't Stop?

Here are some suggestions if the "talkers" don't wind down:

1. Say "thank you" to the person talking and ask if anyone else has something to add.
2. Call on someone to read the Scripture given in the study.
3. Have everyone find and read additional Scriptures.
4. Go on to the next question.
5. Say, "The study seems to be at a standstill. Let's get it moving again." Be bold, yet tactful. Give a little, but don't forget you have to take the initiative to keep the study moving.

Often a Bible study is the only social outlet for women. They need to talk; they are lonely. You have to be sensitive to allow those with needs to express themselves, but yet the quiet ones have needs too. Pray about this. Ask for discernment and wisdom.

Be Bold As a Lion

If it becomes necessary, have an honest confrontation with the domineering woman. Ask her to lunch and then in loving and plain words tell her that you appreciate her enthusiasm in the group and her ability to talk, but that it's your responsibility to "draw out" the quiet women. Ask her if she would help by being sensitive and not contributing to every conversation; and when she does talk, to limit her conversation.

Perhaps she won't come back to the study. She might be offended. That's the risk you have to take. But one domineering person can ruin the study for all, and it isn't fair to the others.

Tape a Session

If straying from the topic and excessive talking by one or two are problems, you may wish to tape record a group session. Have a special meeting to listen to the tape as a group with the purpose being to analyze the ratio between discussion of study material and general "talking." This can be a real eye opener. You may hear your voice more than you should. Leaders can dominate, too.

What About Those "Quiet" Ones?

I call them the invisible ones. They never say a word or contribute a thing.

Again, use your eyes—this time to encourage speaking! Give them attention. This gives them a feeling of affirmation and acceptance. Talk to them. Ask them what they think, what they feel, if they have anything to add. Smile at them, urge them on. Before long, they will be involved.

Also, try to remember something each of the shy ones brings forth; then, when possible, try to call attention to it in the discussion later, or personally to them after the meeting. This will give them a feeling of importance, self worth, and belonging.

CHAPTER 11

A Man's Viewpoint

Not that I have already obtained this or am already perfect; but I press on to make it my own, because Christ Jesus has made me His own (Phil. 3:12).

Darrell is a real estate salesman. He is gifted in evangelism. He shares the good news of Jesus Christ whenever the Lord makes an opportunity.

But back when he was a new Christian, God needed him for something else. Darrell happened to be in the right place at the right time; there was a group of people God wanted to reach. Darrell doesn't think of himself as having the gift of teaching, but out of obedience to the Spirit's urging, he taught. The following is his story.

Darrell's Story

I had been a Christian for about a year and a half when I began to get an inner urging to start a men's Bible study. I felt it should be on how to become a mature man in the Lord. I wanted a study where Christ was the reason for gathering, and one where we could share the joys and trials of our spiritual walk. Because I had been unchurched before my conversion, it was important to me that the group be interdenominational. My thoughts were to first establish a core group of Christians, then invite friends and neighbors who were not believers.

There were many questions running through my mind . . . "How should I start? Where will we meet? When will we meet? What will we study?" I began to pray for guidance.

In my heart I was being asked some questions too. It was like God was saying, "Are you willing to let Me lead you? Will you allow Me to bring the group together? Are you willing to receive and love those I send?"

As I submitted myself to God with, "Yes, Lord, I'm willing," He began to answer my questions.

The first answer came when I found the "right" study book. *The Measure of a Man,* by Gene A. Getz (Glendale, Calif.: Gospel Light Regal Books, 1974) is a bible study of Christian characteristics and qualities of maturity as found in 1 Timothy

3:1–7 and Titus 1:5–9. As I previewed the book I found that this was exactly what I needed in my own life: "To learn from God's Word and from others in the study how to become a more mature man of God."

As outlined in the book, there were twenty characteristics and qualities of maturity specified by the apostle Paul. These would be the basis of the study as well as the number of weeks we would meet.

I decided to follow the author's suggestions to meet in the morning before work. What a way to start the day! I talked to the owner of a local restaurant about the possibility of a group's meeting for breakfast and study once a week. He not only said, "Yes," but suggested, "this is what we need in Prior Lake."

Because of my background I didn't want to have a "religious meeting." But I wanted Christian fellowship with "born again" Christians. Looking back, I realize that I needed the fellowship and growth resulting from "brothers ministering to brothers" as much if not more than the others who came to the study.

Getting Started

Now, how should I start? A friend in advertising suggested I put an ad in the local newspaper. At first I thought that method too impersonal, but after thinking about it, I decided to try it. The ad was placed and read as follows:

CHRISTIAN MEN OF PRIOR LAKE AREA
Discover how to become a more mature man of God. Men's breakfast fellowship will begin Thursday, Sept. 4, at 6:15 A.M. at Martha's Place. We will study an exciting book *The Measure of a Man*. Come for an hour of study, sharing and growing in God.

There, it was done!

I'm in sales, and I've been trained over the years that success is evident by the "numbers"; the more you sell, the more successful you are.

I began to have doubts and fears that no one would show up for my meeting. I even wondered if I was the only Christian in my little town. But I had committed this study to the Lord, believed it was His idea, and was determined to stand firm, trusting God to send the right people. When I told Satan to "get behind me," the doubt and apprehension left.

The big day arrived. I sat waiting, trying to look calm and trusting. One by one three men arrived—all strangers. As we talked and got acquainted, I realized from what they said that two were Christians and one was not (yet). They all wanted to be part of a group like this, and each one had a friend or two who might be interested.

I had bought the study books, so I distributed

them and we planned to meet the following week to do the first chapter, "How to Recognize A Man of God." We decided that at each meeting we would take thirty minutes to read what the Scriptures had to say about a certain quality, and then follow with thirty minutes of discussion, the focus being on how each of us could better develop that particular quality in our lives.

Although this first meeting was on a Thursday, after talking it over, we agreed that Wednesday would be better so we changed our meeting day.

Our personalities and jobs differed, as did our home situations and life goals, but we had one thing in common—personal struggles and the desire to live a victorious life.

The second week I was pleased to see eight men at the restaurant. This group continued on throughout the study.

This was the sequence I followed each week as leader: I arrived at Martha's Place at about 6 A.M. I prayed for the group and myself while I waited for the others. When they came, about 6:15, I had coffee waiting for them. We opened our study with a brief prayer and got right into our lesson.

We did our lesson and read our Scriptures while we had coffee. I instructed the waitress to take our orders at 6:40, and when our breakfast arrived we were ready to go into the discussion part of the study. We did this while we were eating.

Our study ended with a brief prayer. Sometimes

those who could stay beyond the hour would remain and the discussion would continue.

At the end of each chapter was a personal project of self-evaluation. We did this together. We occasionally discussed our progress with our wives. There were some very pointed questions. These questions helped the men to become candid with each other as they opened their lives and shared their emotions. As opportunities came, we prayed for and ministered to each other.

A Child Is Born

About halfway through the study, Dick told us that God had shown him, through the Scriptures and the Bible study, that he did not have a personal relationship with Jesus Christ. This explained why he had seemed so unsettled and lost. He had been trying to do religious things without the power of a relationship with God through Christ.

Three of us counselled and prayed with Dick for salvation, and after many tears, there was the joy when Dick received assurance that he did indeed have a personal relationship with God through faith in Jesus Christ. The following weeks for our friend were full of joy and victory. He understood that he still would have problems but that none of them were too big for God. He moved back to New York after the study was over and returned to the job he had left at the time when his life became messed up.

As the study neared the end, I could see changes not only in my life but also in the lives of each man involved. God had healed marriages, renewed relationships, torn down barriers, and become more real to each of us. We were learning God's principles and were applying them to our everyday situations with fantastic results. We were becoming victorious, and we all saw many answers to our prayers. Men who had been quiet and reserved found courage to tell others what Christ was doing in their personal lives. Some found boldness to tell others of the plan of salvation. We grew very close and developed brotherly love for one another.

After this study ended, the men wanted to continue. We decided on 1 Corinthians and kept on with our weekly meetings. A fellow joined us who had been eating breakfast at the restaurant, had seen us having a good time together, and was curious about what we did each week.

The restaurant changed ownership, and the new owners were not punctual in opening up in the morning. Soon it closed. We went to another cafe, but conditions were not good, so we prayed for a quiet meeting place. The men commented that they didn't care if they had breakfast or not, but they needed the "spiritual food" to grow.

I had changed jobs and my new supervisor was a Christian. He suggested we use the conference room in his building for our new meeting place. I was still the leader even though I had tried to encourage others to take over.

An Early Morning Surprise

One morning, Dave, a fellow salesman, brought his wife, Elaine, to the study. This was quite a shock to "us men" but the following week another wife arrived. This took a little getting used to as we felt this was a "men's study." But we found that it brought life and variety. Things were happening: answered prayers, people opening their lives to God, changed attitudes, the Scriptures coming alive. Dave and Elaine admitted they were not Christians, but they wanted to find out more about Jesus. They were a real challenge to us. They were good for the group because they caused us to dig into God's word to find answers to their many questions. As they listened to our answers to prayer and as the truth was taught, their interest grew.

After leading the Bible study for two years, I felt I needed a rest. I began more insistently to encourage others to take the leadership. I needed to be part of the group but the duties of leadership were heavy. Was it possible to switch roles in the group after two years? Would they still rely on me for leadership? I asked all of them to pray about it and think individually about taking over the leadership duties. After prayer, no other leader came forth. So I continued guiding the group.

About this time my company changed locations to a smaller building with no conference room. My boss moved out of state, and I took a management position in a branch office. The Lord began to teach me there is a time and a season for His work and that our study was to end.

Reflections

Since the study ended, seven of the members have moved out of the area. I still get together with a few of the men on a one-to-one basis and our friendship, which began several years ago during Bible study, is still growing.

The teaching experience was good for me. Often in those years I had to stop and check myself by asking, "Who is leading this study, God or me?" Sometimes the answer was, "God wants to, but you're in the way." Then I would have to ask Him for forgiveness and submit myself to Him. God prefers the humble.

In retrospect, although I was young in the Lord and did not feel qualified to lead a Bible study, I knew "God was able to supply all my needs" and if He wanted me in a leadership role, He would give me the wisdom and knowledge—as well as the faith—to see it through.

One important thing to remember: I was going to a church where Christ was Lord, and I was continually being taught from the Bible. I was in daily communion with God by reading the Word myself and spending time in prayer. I was receiving from God, and because of this, was able to share with others.

CHAPTER 12

Now What?

As the size of your group increases, you may notice the intimacy you had with the smaller group disappearing. Discussions get very long with each person commenting and adding to the conversation. It becomes increasingly difficult to keep on the track, and once "off," a struggle to get back.

Often you have a sense of concern for one or more of the members, but it is impossible to help them individually. They leave during the farewells, and you never really get to know them.

You notice the "quiet" people become almost invisible, never contributing to the discussions, and two or three people do most of the talking.

Coffee time gets longer and longer, and there is much visiting. This usually happens when you have ten or more in the group.

It's good to try to keep the size of study groups small, but often they grow beyond our control. It happens in this way: You say "Yes" to one person, and soon another drops in. She brings a friend, who tells a pal, who asks her mother, who brings a niece, who invites her sister, who comes with her roommate. The roommate calls a school chum who brings the lady next door.

But the situation can only stretch so far.

The natural result is a "split." To "split" means to divide the group into two or more new Bible study groups. To do this you will need leaders for each new group and a willingness on the part of those attending to break up. You, as leader, should be watching for anyone who exhibits leadership capabilities and encouraging them to consider leading a group.

Groups need to divide if they are to multiply. This is good and correct. But, there is a "right" time to do it.

Don't be in a hurry to divide. You don't want to split up prematurely. There may be some spiritual "babes" who will suffer. If you have brought some to the Lord and they really need you, keep them in your group.

There will also come a time when they should leave your mothering and become part of another group. You will know when that time comes. Remember, our spiritual children have to grow up, too, and we are to encourage that growth. We are not to build a "following." They are to follow Christ, not us.

You Need "Starter"

To make sourdough bread you need "starter" for each new batch, some of the old to put into the new.

You need some of the old group in each new group to be the yeast. If they are all new or "babes," it's too soon to split. You have a responsibility to work with them, nurture them, and get them grounded in the Word. If for some very important reason you can't continue with the group, find another leader, one you know personally as a teacher of the truth—or steer them to another group in your area. Don't leave them stranded.

When You Finish a Study

Whether you "split" or not, take a break.

Often the women are just beginning to know each other. Some have really "caught on" to Bible study and are anxious to start another. Others have had a struggle and really aren't enthusiastic. What do you do?

Have a Party

The week following your last Bible study or

your last meeting, have a party. If your study is in the morning, plan a lunch. If it's an afternoon study, have the group come early for lunch. An evening study can meet an hour early for supper.

With just a little planning you can set up a "pot luck" affair. Each one brings some food to share with the others. But make arrangements so that you don't end up with three pots of pork and beans, five tuna salads, and one apple pie.

For eight people you could have:

1 dessert	2 hot dishes (casseroles)
1 salad (jello)	1 tossed salad
rolls and butter	punch
relishes	

At the meal talk about selecting and doing a new study (see Chapter 2). Let the women know if you are planning to teach another class. Invite them to continue if they wish. If it is possible, continue as leader of your group for about a year. This will give you a chance to do several studies together. Always give the individuals the option of going on to another study. There should be a fresh commitment from the members for each study. Some will go on, others may drop out. Give them the freedom of choice.

Keep the names and telephone numbers of those who don't continue, and when the group starts another study, give them a call and extend an invitation to rejoin.

Make Changes

During this natural break between studies, make any changes you feel would benefit the group. Perhaps you will want to change meeting places, days, or study time. Maybe another person will offer to take the responsibilities of hostess for the next study. Talk this over with the present hostess and learn what she would like to do. Maybe she would prefer someone else's taking the job.

What About Summer Studies?

I usually plan to start a group in the fall, taking a week's break at Thanksgiving, Christmas, and Easter. I plan a one-week break between studies, and I work with the group until the end of May.

It has been my experience that when summer comes and a study is finished, the group wants to go on through the summer. They urge the leader to offer herself for the study, but then the attendance goes way down. Everyone has good intentions to attend, but with children out of school, vacations, and summer fun, it's a problem.

The group members have good excuses for missing the sessions, but the leader has to come whether anyone else shows up or not.

One solution, if your group is not a new believers' study, is to use teaching tapes and a cassette recorder. The group or whoever comes listens to the tapes and has a brief discussion. This can be done without a leader if someone will open and close with prayer. Using this approach there is no homework and you feel more free to drop in.

There are many excellent tapes available on many topics. Be sure your pastor, priest, or elder approves of the ones you use. Just because someone has taped a message doesn't mean he is correct in his doctrines and beliefs.

Leaders Need To Learn Too!

As leaders you need to be diligent in your personal study and reading of the Bible. In order to "give" each week, you need to take in something to give.

If you notice yourself beginning to feel "empty," check out your spiritual "intake." Study the Bible. Go to a retreat. Listen to Christian radio. Invest in a series of Bible messages on cassettes and listen to them as you work around your home.

I belong to several tape libraries and get tapes from all over the country. The speakers are pastors, priests, and other dynamic leaders who teach me from the Word of God. Investigate what is available from your Christian bookstore and church library. Ask your pastor if he has any books he would recommend. Read about great men of faith: Smith Wigglesworth, Norman

Grubb, Praying Hyde, C. S. Lewis, Rees Howells, and others.

If you attend a church that has special guest speakers and evangelists—go hear them. Be a learner too!

Also, it's important that you learn to say no. Often you're the kind of person who wants to take on too many good things. Don't stretch yourself too far.

CHAPTER 13

A Letter to Leaders

Dear Reader,*

. . . you are like a son [daughter] to me in the things of the Lord. May God our Father and Jesus Christ our Lord show you his kindness and mercy and give you great peace of heart and mind.[1]

Here are my directions: Pray much for others; plead for God's mercy upon them; give thanks for all he is going to do for them.[2] Don't waste time arguing over foolish ideas and silly myths and legends. Spend your time and energy in the exercise of keeping spiritually fit. Bodily exercise is all right, but spiritual exercise is much more impor-

***Scripture verses quoted from 1 and 2 Timothy in this chapter are taken from *The Living Bible* (Wheaton, Ill.: Tyndale House Publishers, 1971) and are used by permission.**

tant and is a tonic for all you do. So exercise yourself spiritually and practice being a better Christian, because that will help you not only now in this life, but in the next life too. This is the truth and everyone should accept it. We work hard and suffer much in order that people will believe it, for our hope is in the living God who died for all, and particularly for those who have accepted his salvation.

Teach these things and make sure everyone learns them well. Don't let anyone think little of you because you are young. Be their ideal; let them follow the way you teach and live; be a pattern for them in your love, your faith, and your clean thoughts.[3]

Take your share of suffering as a good soldier of Jesus Christ, just as I do, and as Christ's soldier do not let yourself become tied up in worldly affairs, for then you cannot satisfy the one who has enlisted you in his army. Follow the Lord's rules for doing his work, just as an athlete either follows the rules or is disqualified and wins no prize. Work hard, like a farmer who gets paid well if he raises a large crop. Think over these three illustrations, and may the Lord help you to understand how they apply to you.[4]

Steer clear of foolish discussions which lead people into the sin of anger with each other. Things will be said that will burn and hurt for a long time to come.[5]

Again I say, don't get involved in foolish arguments which only upset people and make them angry. God's people must not be quarrelsome; they must be gentle, patient teachers of those who are wrong. Be humble when you are trying to teach those who are mixed up concerning the truth. For if you talk meekly and courteously to them they are more likely, with God's help, to turn away from their wrong ideas and believe what is true. Then they will come to their senses and escape from Satan's trap of slavery to sin which he uses to catch them whenever he likes, and then they can begin doing the will of God.

You may as well know this too, [Friend], that in the last days it is going to be very difficult to be a Christian. For people will love only themselves and their money; they will be proud and boastful, sneering at God, disobedient to their parents, ungrateful to them, and thoroughly bad. They will be hardheaded and never give in to others; they will be constant liars and troublemakers and will think nothing of immorality. They will be rough and cruel, and sneer at those who try to be good. They will betray their friends; they will be hotheaded, puffed up with pride and prefer good times to worshiping God. They will go to church, yes, but they won't really believe anything they hear. Don't be taken in by people like that.

They are the kind who craftily sneak into other people's homes and make friendships with silly, sin-burdened women and teach them their new doctrines. Women of that kind are forever following new teachers, but they never understand the truth.[6]

But you must keep on believing the things you have been taught. You know they are true for you know that you can trust those of us who have taught you.[7]

The whole Bible was given to us by inspiration from God and is useful to teach us what is true and to make us realize what is wrong in our lives; it straightens us out and helps us do what is right. It is God's way of making us well prepared at every point, fully equipped to do good to everyone.

And so I solemnly urge you before God and before Christ Jesus—who will some day judge the living and the dead when he appears to set up his kingdom—to preach the Word of God urgently at all times, whenever you get the chance, in season and out, when it is convenient and when it is not. Correct and rebuke your people when they need it, encourage them to do right, and all the time be feeding them patiently with God's Word.

For there is going to come a time when people won't listen to the truth, but will go around looking for teachers who will tell them just what they want to hear. They won't listen to what the Bible says but will blithely follow their own misguided ideas.

Stand steady, and don't be afraid of suffering for

the Lord. Bring others to Christ. Leave nothing undone that you ought to do.[8]

May the Lord Jesus Christ be with your spirit.[9]

Farewell,
Paul

May God bless you. And may He give all who desire it the "gift" of teaching.

In His Love,
Norma

[1] 1 Timothy 1:2, TLB.
[2] 1 Timothy 2:1, TLB.
[3] 1 Timothy 4:7-12, TLB.
[4] 2 Timothy 2:3–7, TLB.
[5] 2 Timothy 2:16,17, TLB.
[6] 2 Timothy 2:23-26—3:1–7, TLB.
[7] 2 Timothy 3:14, TLB.
[8] 2 Timothy 3:16,17—4:1–5, TLB.
[9] 2 Timothy 4:22, TLB.